The Jesus Path:

The Eightfold Journey

of Spiritual Discovery

The Jesus Path:

The Eightfold Journey

of Spiritual Discovery

By Stephen Poos-Benson

Dedication

To my father
George L. Benson

As always . . .
Phoebe Poos-Benson

Acknowledgements

I am blessed with a group of people who encouraged, guided, and supported the effort of bringing *The Jesus Path* to publication. Their commitment to the project made it happen.

My first thanks are to my wife Phoebe. She is a constant support of my work and writing. She affords me the time and space I need to be creative. She is my life, my love, and my best friend.

This book would not have happened without my friend and editor Kathy Brown. Kathy spent hundreds of hours pouring over each line of *The Jesus Path*. She taught me how to write with passion and inspiration. Kathy encouraged me to find my voice and inspired me to bring it to fruition. If you're reading *The Jesus Path,* it's because of Kathy's work. Thank you, thank you, Kathy.

Several people read *The Jesus Path* and offered their insight. My thanks go to John Rankin, Jane Ritterson, Mark Bigelow, Suzan Leach, Mary Benson, Terri Townsend, and Betsy Rehling.

I also want to thank the members and friends of Col-umbine United Church who gave me a sabbatical, so I could write the initial drafts of *The Jesus Path*. We have had an amazing thirty-five-year journey together.

My thanks go to my creative partner Mitch Samu. Mitch has been a cheerleader, a challenger, and a constant source of encouragement.

To all my friends and colleagues, you are a blessing. Please hear my thanks for all you do to inspire me in my life and work.

The Jesus Path

Table of Contents

Introduction

I want you to have a joyful life with meaning, hope, and satisfaction. It is my prayer that you experience and celebrate the presence of God.

I believe following Jesus brings us this joyful life. Following his path opens us to depths of personal understanding, stronger interpersonal relationships, and a way to interact with God. It allows us to explore and discover new spiritual depths.

However, I think we've made Jesus too complicated. Like conflicting road maps, volumes of dense texts and sacred books were written on how to follow Jesus. Some so complex, it takes advanced academic degrees and knowledge of several languages to understand and interpret these books. Because of this complexity, I believe many turn away from following Jesus and fail to develop a relationship with God.

Jesus said it very clearly; "There are two great commandments; love the Lord your God with all your heart, soul, mind, and strength, and the second is like it, and love your neighbor as yourself" (Matthew 22:37-39). He then simplified it yet again, "A new commandment that I give you, love one another" (John 13:34). Love, it's that simple. If we take Jesus's message of love and apply it to our lives, we are following him. But sadly, from these simple verses we have created a vast religion—Christianity.

Would we be inspired to follow Jesus if we found a simpler way of understanding his message? I believe there is. I desire to present Jesus in a more accessible way to all of us. There's nothing complicated about this book—no great theology or biblical interpretations, just a simple explanation of how to follow Jesus.

I did not write this with the scholar or theologian in mind. This is written for the beginner who contemplates following Jesus for the first time. Or perhaps to someone who's followed Jesus their whole life but has never been able to sort out their faith in any organized fashion.

Yet, in its simplicity, I'm writing an introduction to Jesus from a progressive perspective meaning using the most contemporary insights from many schools of thought that point us towards a forward-thinking, *progressive* understanding of Jesus.

Many introductions for following Jesus are from a conservative viewpoint. I feel these introductions give people a narrow understanding of Jesus, the Bible, and living the Christian life. I hope to show people at the onset that learning to follow Jesus means using all the tools available to us; historical studies, social and scientific insights, and alternative spiritual thoughts. However, to be balanced, I want to show the significant differences between progressive insights and a more evangelical view.

As a progressive, I'm very committed to using non-sexist language as it relates to the name of God. At times, this leads to cumbersome syntax when referring to "God" multiple times in the same sentence. At times, I leave the reference the same. For example; "God spoke to Abraham and *God* said . . ." instead of, "God spoke to Abraham and *he* said." Other places I alternate the pronouns for God, "He," and "She." My intention is to model a progressive view of God where *God* is more than a masculine persona.

The book introduces eight paths to build a relationship with Jesus. Why eight? The Eightfold Path of Buddhism has always inspired me. I've studied Buddhism for several years and find it to be a complex set of beliefs. But if you boil Buddhism down to its basic tenets, there are the Four Noble Truths and the Eightfold Path. This path is simple and clear, and I've asked myself, "Why not do the same for Jesus?"

After contemplation and talking with others, I narrowed it down to what I believe are the eight essential paths needed to follow Jesus. Are there more than eight? Of course, there are, there are probably dozens, I chose these paths because they are the ones I follow. And this is a crucial point—*in my own life*. They are the product of my own spirituality.

The stories about myself are authentic to provide a personal account of my faith journey. In many ways, this book is the story of my pilgrimage with Jesus. I share my spiritual highs where I have felt the divine presence of God, as well as those times when I felt lost and abandoned. I hope from my own experiences; you see that you don't need to be a spiritual giant to follow Jesus, just an average person seeking to find meaning and hope in the midst of life.

The examples in this book are true stories from those I've met and worked with during my thirty-five years as a pastor. They're people who have traveled the Jesus Path. Some found joy; others ran into severe obstacles. However, each of them has been faithful to their journey. To protect their identity, I changed their names. In a few instances, I created composite identities, merging different stories to make a point.

While each path stands alone, they also weave together like a colorful tapestry. I encourage you to read each chapter in sequence beginning with, "My Story" and concluding with "The Path of Resurrection."

There are questions at the end of the book for further contemplation or use in a group study. I want you to understand there is more to following Jesus than just my insights and ideas. I feel disagreements are not unchristian and create healthy dialogue.

I'm aware there are those who will disagree with what I have to say. They will describe this book as a spiritual dead end. Bless them. I hope my story encourages conversation.

I wrote this book with one simple desire, to inspire you to follow Jesus. By doing so, you will have the abundant life he describes.

Chapter One: My Story

To begin our pilgrimage on the Jesus Path, I'd like to share my journey. It is a crooked path, but one I've always followed.

I have been a Christian my whole life, although not always willingly. Raised in a Presbyterian Church in San Diego, California, I hated every minute of it. I hated dressing up, sitting in church, and listening to boring sermons. To endure the worship services that went on and on and on, my brother and I had "holding your breath" contests. We counted bald heads. We pinched each other as hard as we could. We tried to touch the lady's fur coat in front of us to make her think a fly had landed on her. As soon as the service was over, I bolted for the door.

In Junior High, a brutal church fight in the mid-1960's split our church. It was between those who called themselves "Charismatics" who prayed with their hands in the air praying in tongues, versus the traditionalists; who prayed with their hands in their laps and used their tongues to speak regular words.

My Junior High Sunday school reflected the chaos in the church. I endured the class as long as I could. I listened to teachers tell me I was full of sin and needed to accept Jesus as my lord and savior or I was going to hell. Following my teacher's instructions, I accepted Jesus as my savior at least thirteen times. None of my confessions of faith stuck. As soon as the teachers started talking about sin, I started thinking about sex, and I knew I was lost. So, once again they would tell us to accept Jesus and I would, again, and again, and again. Finally, one Sunday it dawned on me, "Is this who Jesus is? Is this what God is all about? Do I want to be a part of it?" As an eighth-grader, I said, "No." I walked out and waited for my parents in the car. I told them, "I'm never going back." Fortunately, my parents left that church.

Throughout high school, I attended different churches in deference to my parents as they tried to find a new church home. As for me, I was through with God. However, God was not through with me.

When I was a freshman in college, one Friday evening I went to the movie *Godspell*, the classic Christian musical from the 1970's. I was transfixed from the opening scene. As I watched the musical portrayal of the life of Jesus, he became alive. His teaching gripped me, and I was inspired by his message. I was moved by his presence. When Jesus was crucified and died, I had a lump in my throat. At the resurrection, as the characters sang, and Jesus rose, something stirred deep in my heart. I felt a divine hand touch me. I pointed to the screen and said, "*That*, whatever *that* is, whoever *he* is, whatever *it all means*, I want that. I want my life to be like that." Like a wave, an overwhelming feeling washed over me, and before I knew it, I was crying. Those fighting over Jesus in my childhood church missed his message. As I sat in the movie theater, I knew following Jesus was the way I wanted to live.

Within two months I had a dream one night in my college dorm. Jesus stood before me and pointed. He said, "You will be a minister to my people." When I awoke from the dream, my first thought was, "You've got to be kidding. Jesus, I love you and all, but I hate church, I hate ministers, and you've got the wrong guy." But the feeling persisted. I switched majors in college and told people I was going to become a minister. That's when I ran into trouble.

The simple, personal, Jesus I found in *Godspell* was lost in the academics, theological wrangling, and biblical debates. The more I talked with those who called themselves Christians, the more my confusion deepened. I found them to be rigid, judgmental, strict, and unforgiving people. I knew I wanted to follow Jesus, but I also knew I didn't want to be like them. So, I hung on to the notion of my *Godspell* Jesus and kept searching. In seminary, I was introduced to the complexity of Biblical studies and the depth of theology. I studied denominational systems and procedures. I worked hard and dedicated myself because I knew God had called me.

With all my knowledge, the simple Jesus in *Godspell* was still missing. Over the next several years as a pastor, I tried to find him again. There were dry times when I felt that if there ever was a Jesus in Christianity, he left long ago and all that remained was a brittle religion.

However, Jesus started showing up again. He came to me in visions and dreams. I heard Jesus when I prayed. I saw Jesus on the faces of people. I felt Jesus when I preached. I sensed his presence when listening to people. Instead of being a character in a book, or a religious figure, Jesus became real. Jesus led me to God.

I worked to set aside the precepts of a denomination and the doctrines of a religion. I tried to pay attention to the man and what he said. I patterned my life after his. I wanted his way to be my way, his truth to be my truth, and my life like his life. By trying to live like Jesus, God's presence surrounded me. It was a blessing beyond all blessings. The blessing was so great I started teaching others how to find their way to God through Jesus.

As I taught people to follow Jesus, I discovered the blessing of the faith community we call the church. With each passing year, my love for the church deepened. I began to understand what Paul meant when he taught that the church was the body of Christ.

Church members are Jesus's arms, legs, mind, and voice. When people in the church love others, the love of Jesus becomes real.

When teaching people about Jesus, I realize I am in a long line of those who came before me. My instruction material is not new. I stand on the shoulders of brilliant, faithful, teachers and scholars.

Christianity can be a complicated religion. I have two advanced degrees as well as a doctorate. I've been a pastor for thirty-five years and still don't completely understand what Christianity is all about. When I try to follow Christianity, I get lost in religion. When I follow Jesus, I find God.

This book tells in simple terms what I feel is the Jesus way. I want people to know that when they follow the Jesus Path, they discover the presence of God.

Chapter Two: It Begins
with Jesus

He lived, taught, and according to some, performed miracles. It's amazing that a peasant carpenter from Nazareth had a vision of God that changed the course of history. Yet, that is what this man, Jesus, did. He captivated the lives of millions of followers. For the past two centuries, people embraced his vision to draw near to God. Who is this man Jesus?

Let me introduce you to the Jesus I know. We'll begin with Jesus's father and mother, Joseph and Mary. They were simple people—illiterate peasants. Joseph was a day laborer, perhaps a carpenter or stonemason. As was the custom, their families arranged their marriage. Joseph may have been in his mid- to late-twenties, maybe even his early thirties and Mary may have been in her early- to mid-teens.

Joseph and Mary lived in Nazareth, a rocky hillside village. It was off the beaten path not known for trade, culture, or commerce. Joseph and Mary raised their family in this village. The insignificance of Nazareth played a significant role in Jesus's life. Later in his story, people wonder how such a dynamic man could come from such a lowly town.

The birth of their first-born son, Jesus, is the subject of so many contemporary traditions that it's hard to ferret out exactly what happened. When thinking about the significance of Jesus's birth, I remember he was born into a family of a poor young couple and was as important as a baby born into any family. I like to imagine that Mary and Joseph's love for him wasn't because he was going to be the Messiah or the Christ. These titles ascribed to him later had little bearing on what his parents felt about him. As their first-born child, he was cherished.

Jesus had a number of siblings. The gospels and later letters refer to anywhere from three to eight brothers and sisters. As the gospels tell the story of Jesus, very little is written about his early childhood. Luke tells us he was a provocative twelve-year-old who challenged the most learned men in the temple. After his childhood, Jesus falls off the historical map. We know very little if anything with accuracy about his adolescence, his early adult years, and how he lived until he began his ministry at the approximate age of thirty-three.

Some fantastic legends exist describing his teens and early adulthood as he traveled to distant lands in the Far East and India. Supposedly, he learned philosophy and became enlightened and then returned to his homeland sharing what he learned. Others believed he stayed in Nazareth and was educated as a rabbi preparing him for his great ministry. I have a more mundane, yet profound understanding of Jesus's missing years. However, remember that my belief is also conjecture, based on the studies of others.

At some point in his life, his father Joseph drops out of the story. He was present at Jesus's birth, conceived other children, and created a household he supported as a laborer. It may be assumed because he was older than Mary and the physical challenge of his profession, he died before Jesus matured as an adult. If this were true, then Jesus, as the firstborn, would be the head of the house and supported his mother and younger siblings. As was the custom, he would take over the family business and follow in his father's footsteps by becoming a tradesman, day laborer, stonemason, or as tradition ascribes, a carpenter.

As the head of the household, Jesus was responsible for raising and caring for his siblings until either marriage or a vocation supported the youngest. Bound by the cultural mores, Jesus postponed any personal longings or visions until he fulfilled his familial responsibilities.

Jesus attended the local synagogue with his family. His education was in the Jewish faith and ways of the world. Throughout his early adult years, he may have shown the acumen for the more complex depths of the Jewish faith. If Luke's tradition bears truth, then Jesus's innate curiosity may have blossomed into a brilliant intelligence by his adult years. Because of his keen insight; along with his familial responsibilities, it is possible he was set aside and groomed to become a rabbi. Hence, when he begins his ministry, his followers called him by the reverential title, "Rabbi" meaning, "Teacher."

Jesus lived at the apex of the major trade routes. Global commerce from Asia and India passed by his doorstep on its way south to Egypt. The Jewish people were clannish and kept away from gentiles, or any outsiders, for fear of religious uncleanliness. However, it is safe to assume the trade routes brought merchandise, philosophies, and theologies from distant lands. These ideas could have easily filtered into the general population and may have piqued the interest of a creative and innovative Jesus.

Through the teachings of the synagogue, his interaction with foreign ideas, his own creative, brilliant, and innovative mind, or a combination of all three; Jesus developed a captivating and compelling vision of God.

There was some event in Jesus's life that suddenly released him from his familial responsibilities, allowing him to begin his public ministry. Maybe his last sibling was married off, or he completed his education and training as a rabbi, but something propelled him out to the local community.

Jesus began teaching his vision of God. The peasants living in the area were immediately captivated. He gathered disciples to study under him; with scores of others following him as he traveled throughout the countryside. Jesus taught that God was immediately available to them. They didn't need to go to the Temple to experience the presence of God. God was as close as the birds in the air and the lilies of the field.

His teachings were not attractive to everyone. Jesus's view of God was diametrically opposed to the traditional teachings of the local synagogue, the temple in Jerusalem, and its local representatives—the Pharisees. As the gospels portray, Jesus was repeatedly in conflict with these groups—and frequently thrown out of the synagogues where he taught. The Pharisees took umbrage with Jesus when he questioned their authority. The Pharisees were like your local pastor: professional, educated teachers of the temple, who lived among the people assuring their laws and beliefs were taught and practiced. As educated as they were, Jesus taught that their highbrow standards were an affront to God and people needed to dismiss them altogether.

At this point in Roman history, Palestine was a small backwater area of little concern. However, for centuries the Jewish people were intent on driving the Romans from their land. Small bands of Jews called Zealots took up arms to force them out. They dreamed of a pure nation devoted to their God. Some began to call Jesus the Messiah of God. This Messiah was to fulfill two critical prophecies: first to reform the Temple, and second, to purge the Roman occupying forces from the land. Many of his followers and one of his disciples urged Jesus to take up arms against the Romans to fulfill the Messianic prophecies as written in the Hebrew Bible. However, Jesus had other ideas. He encouraged people to shift their attention from fighting the Roman Empire to focusing on the kingdom of God.

While Jesus was popular with the people during his three-year ministry, he first became a nuisance to the religious elite, and then an out-and-out threat to their legitimacy. If Jesus was indeed the long-awaited Messiah, it meant he would reform the Temple in Jerusalem by casting out all the Temple leaders. His life was threatened when he took his ministry to Jerusalem, and his popularity grew.

Similar stories of how Jesus was killed are told in the Gospels. Temple authorities arrested Jesus on trumped-up charges. Tried by a kangaroo court and convicted, he was handed over to the Roman authorities for execution. While many people think the Jews killed Jesus, it's important to note that this is not the case. The vast majority of the Jewish population was supportive of Jesus and his vision of God. Only the Jewish authorities opposed his message. Jesus was such a threat to them they conspired with Pilate, the Roman Governor, to have Jesus executed.

The Romans had their reasons for killing Jesus. He stood against the claims of the Roman Empire that they were the kingdom of God. The Romans crucified him, not because of what the Hebrew religious elite believed–but for sedition. The Romans viewed Jesus as a social agitator who would not be tolerated. His crucifixion was to frighten and intimidate his followers. They beat him, took him to a nearby hill, and crucified him. (Dominic Crossan explains the causes of Jesus death in his book, *Who Killed Jesus? Exposing the Roots of Anti-Semitism in the Gospel Story of the Death of Jesus*, Harper Collins, 1996).

Following his death, a few of Jesus's followers took his body down from the cross. They bathed him, anointed his body with spices and wrapped him in a shroud. Taking his body, now prepared for burial, they laid him in a tomb and sealed it with a large stone. If he was the Messiah, all hopes died with him.

Three days later the world changed.

It's called the resurrection. The stories describing this event are compelling. Opinions differ on what happened; some said Jesus was physically raised from the dead three days after his burial. Others disagreed and said his resurrection was a spiritual event. Many said it was a hoax. Whatever happened, it was profound and changed all his followers. While some were confused and doubted what had happened, others were filled with passion. Maybe Jesus was indeed the Messiah, the Son of God.

The resurrection was so extraordinary that within a few years it started a movement. It wasn't a religion with doctrines, dogmas, and Holy Scriptures, but people compelled by Jesus's vision. They called themselves, "The Way." Inspired by God's spirit, they were compelled to spread the news of Jesus's vision and what happened at his resurrection. They claimed that Jesus was indeed the Messiah. But their understanding of his messianic role differed from what the scriptures foretold. The temple he purified wasn't the one in Jerusalem, but the temple of people's hearts. The empire he ushered in was not to conquer the Romans; it was the Kingdom of God transcending earthly boundaries.

Their message was vibrant and drew significant crowds who joined The Way. They were young and old, peasants and wealthy. Together they started a two-thousand-year movement that touched the lives of countless millions of people taking us to where we are today.

Chapter Three: The Path of Joy

It begins with joy. Some may find this strange. Shouldn't we start by talking about the Bible, prayer, sin, or salvation? No, I believe following Jesus starts with joy.

The joy of following Jesus looks and feels differently at various times. Sometimes joy is a complete lightness in our soul—the joy connecting us to God. Other times joy buoys our spirits. It puts a smile on our faces and gives us a feeling of contentment. Other times, joy fills us with happiness and laughter.

Jesus and Joy

Jesus came to bring us joy. He said, "I have said these things to you so that my joy may be in you, and that your joy may be complete" (John 15:11). "You have pain now, but I will see you again, and your hearts will rejoice, and no one will take your joy from you" (John 12:22). "Ask, and you will receive, so that your joy may be complete" (John 16:24). "I speak these things in the world so that they may have my joy made complete in themselves" (John 17:13).

Joy, joy, joy, it's everywhere in the teachings of Jesus and his followers. Although Jesus's disciples encountered suffering and persecution, the rock-bottom foundation of their faith was joy. The followers of Jesus were those who had smiles on their faces and smiles in their souls.

Jesus loved to bring joy to people's lives. Mary and Martha, two sisters who followed Jesus, were filled with joy when he raised their brother Lazarus from the dead. When Jesus healed a man suffering from mental illness, he worshiped at Jesus's feet and was touched by joy. The healed blind man was joyfully grateful. A woman who had been bleeding for twelve years touched the hem of his robe, and she wept tears of joy. Jesus forgave a woman caught in adultery and she was overwhelmed with joy. Jesus's joy inspired people as they listened to him teach about blessings, about worry, about anger.

Joy filled the gospels stories. Jesus brought joy to us by showing that our God is personal. In the Path of Prayer, I talk about Jesus's relationship with God—he called God, "Father," which is the formal translation of a more intimate name, "Dad, daddy, or Poppa." Jesus turned to his dad on a regular basis. He spent time alone with him. When feeling lost, he prayed to him. As Jesus died on the cross, he cried out to him. God was close and personal to Jesus, and God is the same for us. When we discover that God is intimate, we feel joy because we know that God is not some distant deity in the cosmos, but close, like a friend.

People experience this divine joy in different ways in their life. Consider the following stories.

John came up to me after a worship service and showed me a gold coin. Emblazoned on the coin was the number 15. John, beaming with joy, said, "My AA group gave this to me. It stands for fifteen years of sobriety." He asked if we could pray in thanksgiving for his healing journey. John's joy led him to seek God's presence.

It was a trial for Nancy and Don to get pregnant. They both thought all they had to do was stop using birth control. They never conceived after months of trying. So, they started the process of artificial insemination, which was emotionally, spiritually, and financially draining and endured several failed attempts at fertilization. They could afford only one more round of treatments and this time it was successful. When Nancy and Don came by my office to share their news, they were more than happy; they were filled with joy. But it went beyond their joy, it touched deep feelings in their hearts. Their joy brought them close to God.

Jack felt like he had been in school forever. He followed the traditional education path—elementary, junior high school, high school, college, and a post-graduate degree program. He celebrated every milestone along his journey. But this time it felt different. It may have been the years of challenges or jumping through all the academic hoops that made this final graduation a real celebration.

Standing in his cap and gown, he was filled with anticipation. When he heard "Jack Knottingham," he stepped up the stairs and across the stage. As the provost congratulated him and placed the diploma in his hand, his classmates erupted in applause. In the audience, his parents swelled with pride. For Jack, this was a pinnacle moment and a time of celebration. Jack laughed, did a short happy dance in his black academic gown, and flung his cap into the crowd. It was joy—Jack was full of joy. His family and classmates were also full of joy; I believe God celebrated as well. Somewhere in the heavens God did a quick dance and laughed with Jack. Jack's joy was God's joy.

It was an early summer Sunday morning. Elizabeth woke before her family. She took her mug of Starbucks, walked out on the back patio, and sat in a lawn chair. The morning dew dampened the lawn and clung to the petunias in the flowerbed. Finches were at the feeder and hummingbirds danced above her. She inhaled the coffee's aroma and took a sip. She leaned back in her chair and smiled. Something moved deep within her being. It was joy; simple joy. God feels the same sense of satisfaction that Elizabeth felt. In Genesis, the stories describe that on the seventh day of creation God relaxed, took a break, looked upon the creation and said it was good. As Elizabeth enjoyed her backyard, so God feels the same joy basking in the creation.

Do you experience joy similar to these stories? The possibility of joy surrounds us. Each moment is embedded with a range of feelings to choose from, and joy is one of them. However, it is curious that we often pick frustration, anger, or despair, and skip right over joy. We need to intentionally change our choices. Following the Jesus Path means we choose to fill our lives with joy.

Cranky Christians

Over the years, I found it odd when meeting followers of Jesus who were angry, cranky, frustrated, and vengeful. It puzzles me that some of Jesus's followers are wound as tight as a ball of string. They argue over a range of issues: abortion, gay marriage, immigration, political parties, etc., etc. In their congregations, they fight over which songs to sing, who preaches what, and who sits in what pew. Every time I hear followers of Jesus bicker over these issues I wonder, "Where's the joy?"

How do we bring joy to such complex issues as abortion, gay marriage, and immigration? It's important to remember we are not seeking our joy, but joy for those who are the subjects of our debate; the woman waiting for an abortion, the gay couple who wants their relationship blessed by the church, and the family afraid of deportation. We need to ask, "How does Jesus bring joy to these people and how can we be a part of that joy?" Joy is meant for everyone regardless of sexual reproduction, gender relationships, or nationalities. Jesus's joy embraces everyone.

Jesus brought joy when he freed us from stifling legalism. In Jesus's era, the Jewish religion dictated many laws. Many of these laws separated people from God. Jesus showed a different way; there were no rules and laws keeping people from God. The same is true for us.

Today many of Jesus's followers develop their own sense of laws and legalisms. They demand people follow Jesus in ways only prescribed by them. If Jesus were alive today, he would also break their laws. He would go beyond the legalism and fill people with joy.

When we follow the joy taught by Jesus, it allows us to engage in some of the deepest spiritual practices: compassion and forgiveness.

Joy and Compassion

We discover joy when serving others. Jesus taught that if we're going to find ourselves, we need to lose ourselves. We lose ourselves by dedicating ourselves to compassion—which is discussed later in the book. I think it's important to mention compassion here as well because it is by caring about others that we find joy.

Jesus continually showed compassion. Once there were over five thousand people listening to him teach. When it came to the dinner hour, he realized they were hungry. The gospel describes that he had compassion upon them (Matthew 15:32). Another time Jesus came upon a large group of people, many who were sick and ill. The Gospels say he had compassion upon them and healed the sick and lame (Matthew 14:14). If Jesus came to bring us joy and showed compassion, there is a connection between the two.

There is something about taking time to serve the needs of others that brings joy. God gave us an abundance of gifts, skills, and abilities. When we use them for others, we find meaning in life. When we use our gifts to serve others, we find joy. There is joy in generosity and kindness.

Have you ever served food at the local homeless shelter? Have you ever used a hammer to build a Habitat for Humanity home? Have you taken a meal to someone who was sick or ill? If so, then you know the joy that comes with compassion. Discovering the joy of following Jesus means we serve other people.

Joy and Forgiveness

It's hard to forgive. When someone has done us wrong, we hold onto the pain. However, when we refuse to forgive, we fill our lives with spiritual poison. And this poison affects our spiritual well-being. Our souls begin to sour; our outlook on life becomes clouded with anger and despair. There's an old saying that when we refuse to forgive, it is like drinking poison hoping the other person dies. The only way to cleanse ourselves is to engage the process of forgiveness.

Jesus taught about forgiveness—we need to constantly forgive those who wronged us. In the same way that God forgave us, so are we to forgive. Jesus knew that refusing to forgive destroys our wellbeing. As we walk the Jesus Path, we need to be people of forgiveness.

The process of forgiveness is often long, requiring patience and insight. However, when you're able to let go of the anger and forgive someone, you discover a deep and profound joy. You're no longer holding onto a grudge or resentment. Instead, you have a feeling of lightness, happiness, and joy. While it's not necessarily a joy sending you laughing and skipping down the road, it's a joy that touches the depths of your soul. Forgiveness is a spiritual joy connecting you to God. Joy comes with forgiveness because we know we're following Jesus's teaching. Not only have we cleansed ourselves of the spiritual bile, but we also have joy knowing we're walking the Jesus Path.

Suffering and Joy

But what if you're suffering? What if you're going through trials and hardships? What if the pain and destruction of on-going alcoholism filled John's story? Or what would Nancy and Don's joy be if they hadn't conceived? Would Jack feel joy if he had not passed the exams for grad school? I am not naïve; I know many who battle serious issues in their life. Suffering challenges joy, but it doesn't overwhelm the hope Jesus gave us.

The Jesus who said, "Your joy will be complete," (John 16:24) was also the Jesus who suffered persecution and death by the Temple rulers and the Roman authorities. Yet his persecution and suffering did not stop him from teaching about joy. It's because suffering and pain can lead to joy.

When we endure our suffering, we often feel we're alone. It isolates us from others. But it doesn't have to. Our pain can open us to the suffering of others. Our wounds give us compassion for the wounds of others. When we come together in a community of compassion, we find joy in being with one another.

As people on the Jesus Path, we need to know that suffering, pain, grief, and sorrow are not permanent conditions. You are working through these circumstances. But you're not alone; God is working with you as well. Like a force in a stream pushing against logs and rocks blocking its way, God does the same. These circumstances are not God's final answer for your life. God desires that your life be filled with joy, and God does not stop working until your life brims with hope.

However, in our time of suffering, we need to be intentional when working with God's presence. There are times when we need to architect our joy.

Architecture

A woman named Janet taught me to architect joy. Her husband had a traumatic stroke, and if this devastation was not enough, several years later he took his life. Janet fought her way through this pain each day by doing things that brought her joy; she filled her backyard with flowers, took classes at the community college, and dedicated herself to social justice. She crafted, designed, implemented, and intentionally did things bringing her joy. For Janet, God was never absent; God worked during her circumstances bringing joy to her life. If you're enduring similar pain where there is an absence of joy, you need to follow Janet's example of architecting and implementing your joy. You need to do things that bring you joy.

When talking with people about joy, I ask them what brought joy to their lives. They listed many things including hiking in the mountains, walking on the beach, or sharing a fine dinner with friends. Then I asked when they last did these things. Many said it had been years since doing activities that brought them joy. Jesus can only bring us joy when we intentionally create it.

If you love to listen to music, then fill your life with songs. If you love to read, find books that make you smile. Go to movies, spend time with friends, cook wonderful meals—be intentional. Find the things that make you smile and laugh, and you will find joy. I believe laughter is one of the best expressions of joy.

Jesus, Laughter, and Joy

Did Jesus laugh? The gospels portray Jesus as being very serious. He cursed a fig tree for not bearing fruit. He argued with the Pharisees and condemned their teaching. He healed the sick and raised the dead.

He did serious work. But did he laugh? Did he enjoy a good joke with his disciples? Could he laugh with the children who came to sit on his lap? Were there times Jesus smiled, chuckled, or kicked his head back in a wonderful belly laugh? I believe he did.

If I were to write a gospel, I would tell stories of Jesus laughing. The shortest verse in the Bible is two words, "Jesus wept" (John 11:35). In my gospel, the shortest verse would be, "Jesus laughed."

While it's conjecture on my part, I know Jesus laughed. If he said his purpose was to bring a fullness of joy to our lives, then he had to know happiness. If he knew happiness, then he knew how to laugh.

If Jesus laughed, then following him means we need to laugh. We can laugh at jokes, laugh at life, and laugh with Jesus. If you do a Google search on "Jesus Jokes" you'll find a plethora of stories about Jesus. Some may say these jokes are in bad taste, or they belittle following Jesus. I disagree. I believe Jesus loves to hear these stories and to laugh at himself.

If Jesus could laugh at himself, can we do the same? Sometimes we take ourselves way too seriously. Our faces are stern, our countenance is set, and our jaws are rigid. Life is serious business. But if we never laugh, we're missing a huge part of life. Would our outlook change if we could lighten up and laugh a little at our foibles and mistakes? If we could laugh, then we would find joy. Laughter always leads to joy.

Jesus said to the disciples, "Come follow me." (Matthew 4:19) I wonder if he also had to tell them, "Lighten up. Laugh a little. I've come to bring you joy, happiness, and laughter." I believe following Jesus means we need to learn how to laugh.

Joy and the Resurrection

The Jesus Path leads to joy because of how his life ended. It ended with his resurrection. While this is the last path, we also start here. We begin where we end. After the crucifixion of Jesus, the followers of Jesus put him in a rock tomb. They rolled a huge stone over the opening and sealed it. They said a few prayers, and their hearts broke. They loved Jesus. He was more than a Messiah, he was their teacher, their master, and their friend, and now he was dead. In my work as a pastor, I've seen many dead people. I understand what those followers felt because when you're dead, you're dead. It's over. Your last breath is just that . . . your last breath.

Three days later the women went to the tomb to put spices on Jesus's body. When they arrived, they found the stone rolled away and Jesus's body was gone. What happened was something fantastic. Angels sitting in the tomb told the women that Jesus was alive.

There are many different understandings of what happened in the resurrection. But despite the differing beliefs about the resurrection, the result is joy. The chains of death were broken, a new day dawned. God's ultimate answer for life was not death, but resurrection. The resurrection brings joy.

Practice

We must practice each path, and joy is no exception. To discover the joy that Jesus brings we must engage in the discipline of joy, and it is a discipline.

This discipline says if Jesus came to bring me complete joy, then I'm going to be present in this situation until I discover joy.

Joy requires patience, endurance, and a commitment to the long haul. Joy sometimes comes at the end of a long journey of hard work, illness, or suffering, like Jack working years for his education, John committed to fifteen years of sobriety, or Nancy and Don with in vitro fertilization. But the promise Jesus gives is that we will experience joy, and our joy will be full.

Practicing joy also means that we'll let loose and lighten up. We'll laugh at ourselves and the world around us. While life is serious, we can laugh and smile about a great many things.

Journey

Discovering the joy Jesus brings to our lives is a journey. For some, it comes after years of dedication and work. Others discover it each time they drink their morning coffee.

As followers of the Jesus Path, we are called to empower others to discover joy. We set aside our issues, arguments, and debates. We sacrifice our needs so others may celebrate joy.

Whether your joy is immediate, or a process that takes years, when we follow Jesus, we commit ourselves to joy. If following Jesus doesn't bring you joy, then maybe you need to review what path you're on. Because following Jesus is all about joy. Jesus came to bring you joy, full and complete.

Chapter Four: The Path of the Bible

I'm crazy about the Bible. I love every bit of it. I have an e-Bible but prefer the Bible in book form. I love the leather cover, the gold embossed edges of the pages. I love the heft of it in my hand. I love to open it and just begin reading . . . anywhere. The sacrifices in Leviticus stifle me. I blush when reading the erotic passion in the Song of Solomon. I'm moved when Jesus weeps outside of Lazarus's tomb. My heart aches for Jesus when he hears his cousin, John the Baptist, has been beheaded. I feel the women's fear as they stood outside the empty tomb. I agree with Paul when he chastises the foolish Galatians. The mark of the beast in Revelation spooks me. I open the Bible and hear God speak to me. I lift its pages to my lips and kiss it as I read. It is holy. It is sacred, and I bow before its wisdom.

It hasn't always been this way.

During one of the dark times in my life, I burned my Bible. I did this because tearing it up wasn't enough. I ripped the covers off and tore it page by page. It was a time when I felt abandoned by God. Not that I didn't believe in God, but it was as though God had been there and then walked away. God didn't care. God was a traitor, a liar, and had let me down. If the Bible speaks of God's love, then it is wrong. If God speaks through the Bible, then God stopped speaking to me. God walked away from me, so I would walk away from God. Tearing out the pages was the only way of expressing this pain. When that wasn't enough, I took the pile of pages to the backyard, threw on some gas, lit a match, and watched God's word burn as the tears ran down my face.

It's been thirty-five years since I burned that Bible. I have learned that during our pain God is with us, holding our souls as a mother holds her child. I learned this by returning to the Bible repeatedly, reading and contemplating its words. My faith in God through Jesus has been shaped and formed by the Bible.

Jesus and the Bible

Jesus was wary of scripture. In the early centuries, the Jewish people understood their relationship with God through the Hebrew Bible. What you ate, wore, did, said, and lived was governed by the scriptures. There were Scribes, Lawyers, and Pharisees who interpreted the sacred books. The average He-brew was lost and bewildered in a maze of legalism and laws. Through the legalism of the Scribes and Pharisees, people felt unclean and unwelcomed in God's presence. This legalism made Jesus angry.

Jesus said, "You search the scriptures because you think that in them you have eternal life: and it is they that testify on my behalf" (John 5:39). Jesus wanted to drag their noses out of the scriptures. He wanted them to see that eternal life was not found in reading, interpreting, or adhering to scriptures. Eternal life was found through a relationship with him.

Jesus never wrote a book because if he had, people would have worshipped the book as being holy writ. They would have missed the point.

The point is a person—Jesus. The purpose is a relationship with him. This relationship is living and dynamic. I've been married for thirty-eight years and have three grown children. The five of us love each other. But we also have disagreements. When my kids were teenagers, they baffled me. Now as adults, I'm fascinated as I watch them shape their lives. As a family, we're far from perfect, but we're deeply committed to each other to the point of sacrificing our lives for each other if necessary.

The same is true for a relationship with Jesus. There are times when I love Jesus and times when I'm angry with him. There are times when I'm as baffled with Jesus as I was with my teenagers. There are times when I can only scratch my head and wonder at the things Jesus said and what he meant. I know that his love humbles me, and I desire nothing more than to build a relationship with Jesus. The source of my relationship is the scriptures in the Bible written about him. To know Jesus and his teachings, I go to the Bible. The more I read about Jesus, the more I love the scriptures telling me about him. The more I desire to learn about God, the more I love the pages of the Bible where God speaks to me. My Bible is holy to me because it teaches about the sacred relationship I have with God through Jesus. But I must remember that the Bible is not holy, it's just a book pointing to what is holy—my relationship with Jesus.

The tension between Jesus and the Bible cannot be resolved. If you want to follow Jesus, you need to read the Bible. God speaks through the Bible in a transformative way. This transformation is so profound you are tempted to think the Bible transformed you, and you want to call it holy. It isn't. It is only a book. It is the Spirit of God speaking through the scriptures to you. The Bible is the medium, the tool, through which God speaks, convicts, guides, and teaches those who follow Je-sus.

The Book

Let's look at this book called the Bible. It is handy to download an e-Bible to your phone or tablet, but to become familiar with it you'll need the real thing—a printed book.

When you hold this book in your hands, what do you notice? Is it thick, heavy? Maybe the pages are lined with gold or it may look like an ordinary textbook. The title says, "The Holy Bible." "Bible" is Latin for library. You're holding a holy library. But what makes it holy? We'll cover that below.

The Bible is a confusing book to read. Don't read it cover to cover. It was not intended to be read this way. When someone tells me they've done this, I often wonder why. I admire their commitment, but it confuses their understanding of the Bible. The Bible is not a linear, front-to-back, rendering of what happens over a period of time. The Bible is a mixture of histories, sagas, poems, songs, prophecies, proverbs, letters, and novellas. Each reflects different eras from Israel's history. There is an actual history of the area we call Israel found in history books, but the Bible is not a history book; it's a book *about* a people's history who lived in the land called Israel. It is very important to understand this distinction, but that becomes clearer as we continue our conversation.

As we walk through the Bible, the first thing we find is the table of contents. There are two sections in the Bible, an Old Testament and a New Testament.

First, we need to change the section heading called "The Old Testament." There's nothing old about it. Instead, we will refer to it as "The Hebrew Bible." It is living and dynamic for our Jewish brothers and sisters just as the New Testament is for us.

Run your finger down the chapter headings.

The first five books of the Hebrew Bible are Genesis, Exodus, Leviticus, Numbers, and Deuteronomy. These five books are called the Pentateuch, or the books of Moses. It is one of the most sacred sections of scripture in the Jewish religion.

Then there are the history books: Joshua, Judges, Ruth, 1 and 2 Samuel, 1 and 2 Kings, 1 and 2 Chronicles, Ezra, and Nehemiah. These books are sweeping stories of Israel. They're books filled with love, passion, intrigue, betrayal, war, and murder. They're a great read.

Continue skimming down the table of contents and you'll see Job, Psalms, Proverbs, Ecclesiastes, and the Song of Solomon. These are the poetry books of the Hebrew Bible.

Then come the Prophets; Isaiah through Malachi. These men spoke on God's behalf to those who lived the historical fictions above.

Now open your Bible to the divider between the Old, *Hebrew Bible,* and the New Testament. Some Bibles have a section between the two called, "The Apocrypha." These books cover the four-hundred-year period between the two testaments. The Apocrypha books are significant because they describe the religious culture and the tensions with the Roman Empire that Jesus was born into.

Now turn to the first page of the New Testament, and you'll find the Gospels of Matthew, Mark, Luke, John, and Acts. The order of the gospels is confusing. They are listed first in the table of contents, but these gospels were written forty years after Jesus's life. The letters from Paul should be first. These letters are Romans, 1 and 2 Corinthians, Galatians, Philippians, 1 and 2 Thessalonians, and Philemon.

Next are the books attributed to Paul; Ephesians, Colossians, 1 and 2 Timothy, and Titus. Many readers of the Bible are confused about the authorship of these letters. If the scholars and authorities say Paul wrote these letters, then how can we contradict this? In the first century, it was common practice to write letters in someone else's name to give your writing weight and authority. These letters are important but differ in several ways from the original letters of Paul. We still read them as significant material, but many sections contradict Paul's message of freedom and liberation.

Following Paul's letters are other letters written by assorted people; Peter, James, and John. The gospels were written after these letters. However, when assembling the Bible, the gospels were placed first to tell the stories of Jesus. So, while they're out of historical order, they are first because of their meaning. But it's important to remember that they were written much later than the letters.

After the gospels, we have the book of Acts, which is the second book of Luke. I still wonder why the book of John was inserted between the Luke and Acts. Acts is historical fiction describing the early church.

The Bible ends with the book of Revelation, one of the most misunderstood books in the Bible. Since it's at the end, one would think it's about the end of the world. It's not. It's about the painful period I described earlier in our conversation about the end of the first century when the Romans were destroying Israel. The book of Revelation was written to different churches on how to stay courageous and hopeful in the face of terrible persecution. Its message is that God is with us and never abandons us, which is the perfect message to end the Bible.

The Gospels

The entire Bible is important for our Jesus Path, but the gospels are of particular interest as they tell the stories about him.

I often wish Jesus lived to the age of eighty-five. If he had reached that ripe old age, there would have been plenty of time to record what he said and he believed. We would then have volumes of his teachings. But we don't. There are four gospels written forty to fifty years after he lived. They are beautiful sweeping accounts of Jesus's life. To begin this

Jesus Path, I recommend you start by reading the gospels. As you do, here are few helpful insights

The gospels are not literal accounts of Jesus's life. There was no one following Jesus around with a steno pad copying down every word. Nor are they a transcript of a movie. The disciples and others that followed Jesus relied on oral tradition. Their lives with Jesus were dynamic. The first disciples began telling stories of Jesus after Jesus's death. The two subsequent generations retold and often embellished these stories. As the first-generation eyewitnesses died, the stories were passed down generation after generation. By the last third of the first century, individual church communities developed their unique beliefs based on the context of their own issues. While churches were similar in structure, each wrestled with what it meant to follow Jesus. Near the end of the first century, authors within the communities were compelled to take the oral stories of Jesus and put them in written form.

When you lay the gospels side-by-side notice that they are all similar, yet different. Why are there differences between the four gospels? This question gets at the heart of the meaning of each gospel.

Each gospel was written with the specific needs of a community in mind. Matthew wrote about Jesus addressing the questions his community wrestled with, as did Mark, Luke, and John. The most significant part of each gospel is the title, "The Gospel *according to* Matthew, *according to* Mark, *according to* Luke, and *according to* John." Each church was different, and each gospel author took the stories passed down to them, plus many stories the other authors didn't have. Then they wrote their books *according to* the challenges faced by their churches. This doesn't mean that one gospel is less important than the others; it means that the issues each author faced were significant. The authors wanted the stories of Jesus to be relevant for their people. In the same way we interpret the stories of Jesus for our lives, so did these first authors.

Matthew, Mark, and Luke are called the "Synoptic Gospels." "Syn" is the Greek root word meaning, "Together." "Optic" means "view," as in optic nerve. These three gospels are taken together because they have a similar view. John's Gospel is very different from the other three and is distinct in its message. John's Gospel describes Jesus's universal identity as the Messiah.

Many ask, "Since each gospel tells different stories about the life of Jesus, are some stories more authentic than the others?" There are; some of the lessons and parables accurately retell the history of the man Jesus who lived, while others are an interpretation.

How do you tell the difference? It can be a bit challenging to discern. It's called, "the search for the historical Jesus." As early as the 1880's, scholars have been working to separate the two types of stories. Some stories ring with authenticity, such as the Sermon on the Mount, many of the parables, and the two great commandments to name just a few. Other stories seem out of character with the Jesus who taught about love and forgiveness. For example, there are stories where he rants in anger at different groups of people. And what about the miracles, are they authentic? Again, scholars differ on their interpretation. Does this distinction lessen the authority or impact on our lives? Not at all. It means that we should interpret them for our lives, just as Christians had to do for centuries. To read more about the search for the historical Jesus, I highly recommend, *Meeting Jesus Again for the First time: The Historical Jesus and the Heart of Contemporary Faith,* by Marcus Borg.

Since the gospels are similar with some differences, how do we interpret and apply these gospels to our lives. There are four key concepts to remember when reading the gospels, as well as the entire Bible: Revelation, Inspiration, Application, and Authority.

Revelation

We say the Bible is the revealed Word of God. What does this mean? How does God reveal divine insights? Is the Bible a part of this divine act? First, let's consider what it means to reveal something.

Let's start by asking, "How do you reveal your feelings, insights, and ideas to a person you love?" Over a span of time, you talk to them, use voice inflections, and body language. You tell stories, write poems, and maybe sing songs. You may need to repeat yourself over and over. If you're not getting through to your love, you may need to ask another person to serve as an ambassador on your behalf. You know you have revealed yourself when the object of your affection is inspired to respond in some way.

God faces this tension as well. I believe God is active in the world and our lives. As such, God desires to communicate with us to lead and inspire us. God is actively trying to reveal insights and ideas. But how does God go about this revelation? I think God uses the same tools that we use. At times, God uses a voice, an inflection, and divine body language. To me, a gorgeous sunrise or sunset is God's body language. God must repeat his thoughts until we understand what needs to be revealed.

As followers of Jesus, we say God revealed divine insights through the authors of the Bible. As individuals and communities wrestled with how to lead faithful lives, God was actively revealing new insights as people lived and dealt with their issues. The Bible is the history of this revelation.

As we read the Bible in our contemporary times, is the entire Bible also revealed for us? Some say yes, others say no. I believe and teach that some revelations are what I call historically locked. God revealed the truth to people in particular eras of history. The book of Leviticus is a perfect example. The book is a long list of laws, regulations, and sacrifices on how to be in the presence of God. The book tells us how God revealed divine truths to people of that era but has little to say to us in our contemporary lives. We don't sacrifice animals to purify us so we can stand in God's presence. We love and appreciate Leviticus, but its meaning is historically locked.

The historical sagas of the Hebrew Bible are another example. These stories recount the desire of the Hebrews to be faithful to God's revelation by destroying whole villages and towns in God's name. On God's command, they engaged in battles and warfare. You read these sections and wonder if this is God's divine truth. Does God actually tell the Hebrews to engage in warfare and destroy entire civilizations? No, God doesn't. Instead, we read these sections of the Hebrew Bible understanding them within their historical context. God revealed certain things to the authors living in their era. We read these stories and relish the rich history, but we interpret them for our era.

Then how does God's revelation affect us now? We interpret them by saying these are historically-locked passages about a particular people. However, the timeless message is that God is present during our history. We don't take these passages literally, Instead, we take them seriously and apply them to our contemporary lives.

Other sections of the Bible reveal God's divine truths so that while they speak to someone, they are timeless in their message. The poetry of the book of Psalms is an example. Poems, by their very nature, need to be interpreted. By doing so, their message of God's presence is timeless.

The same is true for the Prophets of the Hebrew Bible. God actively revealed strong messages to these authors for a specific moment in history. Yet through interpretation, we say God's revelation for us is timeless as we wrestle with social issues in our lives.

The gospels ring with this same truth. Each gospel is unique in its revelation. Though each author tells Jesus's story *according to* the needs of their community, the message of Jesus's life is timeless. They reveal how God was working through the life of Jesus.

As followers of Jesus, we say that Jesus was God's ultimate revelation to us. God revealed to us the divine truths of his love and presence through the historical Jesus who lived and walked the earth. The stories of Jesus's revelations were written down in the subsequent generations and recorded in the gospels. Again, the challenge is to interpret the gospels for what they meant then, and then understand what they mean now.

The same is true for Paul's letters, other New Testament writings, and specifically with the book of Revelation. Since Revelation is referred to so much in our contemporary era, let me briefly address its meaning. The book of Revelation is not meant to be taken literally; instead we understand the context it was written for and apply it to our lives. At the end of the first century, the Roman Empire harshly persecuted the Christian churches. The author of the book of Revelation wanted to inspire the Christians of his era to have faith and courage. He chose concepts and images his people would readily understand. The images of the end of the world were often violent and bloody. If we read these passages literally, we think they refer to the end of our world. But when we understand the context of Revelation, we see the author was speaking about the end of the Roman persecution. If we take this book as a literal portrayal of the end of our world it fills us with terror. If we do so, we miss the book's significance for us, as well as those it was written for. As we interpret Revelation we can say the author's message describes God's presence in the midst of pain. Just as they needed to have faith and courage, so do we, knowing that at some point God will bring an end to our suffering.

The ultimate point of God's revelation is that God was actively speaking with the hope they would respond with faith. The question is: was God finished revealing to us when the Bible was concluded or is God still reveling to us now? I believe God is actively revealing divine insights and ideas. I agree with many who say that God is still speaking which is the motto of the United Church of Christ, one of the thirty-three thousand Christian denominations.

The first theme working its way through God's revelation is Inspiration. How did God inspire the authors to write to their people? Were these authors uniquely inspired to record God's revelation?

Inspiration

Writing is magic for me. I sit down and open my head to a deep cosmic pool. Thoughts appear and words typed on a page. Anybody who creates anything, from the crayon scribbles of a second grader in Mrs. Mersdorph's class, to Michelangelo carving the David, to a meal scented with spices, we all dip into this deep pool and take a swim.

All creativity is magic. Comic books, poems, novels, biographies, each author who picks up a pen dives into the magic well. We all come up with different ideas, but it's from the same source.

The magic pool inspires people. The inspiration fills the mind with creative thoughts, colors, and images. Each one who is inspired uses their gifts to give life to the inspiration. I write, a painter paints, and a chef cooks. We're all inspired.

Because I believe in God, I say the magic pool is divine and holy. When I dive into the waters of inspiration, I feel I've touched the face of God. I hear divine whispers. God doesn't dictate what to say, but his holy inspiration propels me forward. My words typed on this page are a result of my swimming with God in the magic pool.

The authors of Matthew, Mark, Luke, and John all went swimming in the magic pool. It's the same pool that Michelagelo, da Vinci, Disney, and Hemingway swam in. Matthew, Mark, Luke, and John touched the face of God; they heard divine whispers, they were driven, inspired to write. But were they taking holy dictation? Was God whispering in their ear telling them exactly what to say about the life of Jesus? No, God doesn't work this way. God doesn't dictate to anybody what to say. The inspired person writes, paints, draws, and cooks, giving expression to their inspiration.

Matthew, Mark, Luke, and John, as well as the hundreds of other writers did the same. They wanted to tell a story about the life of Jesus. They knew some stories about him that others had shared with them. They were brilliant writers. They opened their hearts, dove into the pool and what resulted was magic. The Gospels are magic. The point to understand though is their magic is not any more significant, unique, or divine than anybody else's. They had different gifts as writers, but the result of their inspiration is no greater than the book you're holding.

What drove these authors? Where did they get their insight and inspiration? I believe it was the same thing that has inspired me, God. I feel a divine impulse, a divine inspiration, and a divine ache to communicate with humanity. So did they.

This ache drives me to write my books: I imagine the same ache drove the authors of the Bible to write their stories and insights. We all have the same end desire, that people will be inspired to follow Jesus and develop a relationship with God.

The second theme is on how to interpret the Bible, so God's revelation nurtures my relationship with Jesus and God.

Interpretation

Followers of Jesus who read the Bible are divided into thousands of denominations. Some take the Bible literally, and others take it seriously. It's a concept I've already introduced to you, but let's go further in what it means to take the Bible seriously. Many authors have written extensively about this concept. For additional reading I recommend Marcus Borg's book, *Reading the Bible Again for the First Time: Taking the Bible Seriously but Not Literally.* Let me summarize what Borg and many others believe.

In the extreme, those who take the Bible literally are not open to the intense academic scrutiny of the Bible. They discourage dialogue, doubt, or criticism of the Bible. They interpret the Bible word for word. For them, the Bible is a historical record, a science book, and a day-by-day account of how the world was created. They believe the Bible is perfect because it was a revelation from God.

Recently I walked into a person's home and above their couch in the living room was a huge three-foot sign that said, "God said it, I believe it, that's it." Where was the academic wisdom for this person? Do they willingly put on blinders to all the study and insight that so many faithful followers of Jesus have learned? Are they open to how God continues to reveal knowledge to the faithful today? Do they think the passages from Leviticus apply to them? Was God directing those in the historical sagas to kill people? Is the book of Revelation talking about the end of our world? People who take the Bible literally wrestle with these tensions.

I do not take the Bible literally. I take the Bible seriously and believe God revealed the truth to the biblical authors in given periods of time. While God inspired them, it was unique to their given period of time. It was not intended to be carried down through the ages as eternal divine truths. How do you discern the difference between the two? We do this through academic study and research.

I am committed to the hard, academic study of the Bible. I believe we don't need to turn off our brains when reading the scriptures. We apply every known academic curriculum to this study; history, science, anthropology, sociology, psychology, literary studies, linguistics, and archeology to name a few. We hold nothing back. We doubt, question, and ponder.

After applying these academic studies to the Bible, we start asking questions. Who wrote this passage? Who were they writing to? What issues were they were facing? What did the authors intend to say to their audience? How was God speaking to the Hebrews through the different authors? How is their context similar or different from mine?

Several tools are helpful in this process: a good Bible dictionary, a Bible commentary, and a Bible atlas are valuable as you study and interpret the Bible. There are several online versions that are easily accessible.

As we interpret the Bible seriously and not literally, several contemporary issues are resolved. Here are a few for consideration. By interpreting the Bible, we understand it is not a science or geology textbook. The creation of the world was not done in six days, as described in Genesis, but over millions of years as science teaches. The different species of the world were not created in one of those six days but through a long scientific process of genetics and evolution. By taking the Bible seriously, it allows us to read and interpret the Bible on its own without pitting religion against science. The two complement each other allowing us to study the Bible and science in greater depth.

We've learned that passages telling women to remain silent and subservient to men in the Hebrew Bible and the New Testament speak to a specific era, not to ours. God speaks in profound ways through women. In the church that follows Jesus, women teach, preach, and lead the church.

The Hebrew Bible and the New Testament teach that slavery is an acceptable way of life. We dismissed those passages as historically locked long ago. They speak to a different time and cannot be applied to our contemporary era.

At the writing of this book, the Christian world is debating the issue of Gay, Lesbian, Bisexual, Transgender, Queer, and Inquiring people (GLBTQ). Some say that according to the Bible, these people are an abomination. I join a chorus of people who don't take these passages literally. We take them seriously by saying these passages are historically locked. I believe God blesses the GLBTQ people and reveals divine truth to them just as God did in the past. These people should teach, speak, and lead the church just as straight men and women do. As children of God, their relationships and marriages should be blessed and endorsed by the church that follows Jesus.

Biblical interpretation is an exciting process. When I study different interpretations of the Bible it feels like it's vibrating in my hand. The insights are vast and extensive. I realize how God revealed divine truth several thousand years ago, and how God is doing the same today. As I relish Biblical interpretation, the next challenge is to learn how to apply it to my life.

Application

We can talk about revelation, inspiration, and interpretation for pages, but these are the "academic" concepts of our study. However, if we aren't inspired and feel God's guidance, then who cares? All that work is an academic exercise and while interesting, means nothing. God's purpose in revealing divine truth is to inspire us. To practice this Jesus Path, you need to apply the teachings of the Bible and Jesus to yourself.

Some passages of the Bible are timeless, and I encourage you to begin the process of application with them. The caveat is that they are timeless to me. God revealed divine truth to me and inspired me to act in my life. I only offer them to you as places to begin.

The first place to begin is the two great commandments that Jesus taught, "Love the Lord your God with all of your heart, soul, mind and strength. The second is like it, Love your neighbor as yourself. On these two great commandments hang all the law and the prophets" (Matthew 2:37-40). These verses measure all the other passages. They reveal the divine ultimate truth. The purpose of following Jesus is to love God and your neighbor. If you measure your life by these two laws, ultimately you will follow Jesus.

These two great commandments are derived from the Ten Commandments. Many say they live by the Ten Commandments, but very few can name more than two or three of them. The Ten Commandments are so timeless that many of our contemporary laws and cultural customs are derived from them (Exodus 20:1-17).

Jesus's "Sermon on the Mount" from Matthew's Gospel (Matthew 5, 6, and 7) is inspired. It rings with timeless insight. Jesus teaches us the basics of how to follow him; blessing others through our actions, to not worry, to let go of anger, avoid adultery, and to serve God with joy.

The Prophet Jeremiah says, "For I know the plans I have for you," declares the Lord, "plans to prosper you and not to harm you and to give you hope and a future" (Jeremiah 29:11). This passage reveals God's ultimate desire for us to have a bright and optimistic future. God works in our lives to overcome all obstacles fulfilling this promise.

Paul provided a passage exploring God's love for us in 1 Corinthians, chapter thirteen. Paul writes, "If I speak in the tongues of men and of angels, but do not have love, then I'm a noisy gong and a clanging cymbal . . . Love bears all things, believes all things and hopes all things." This passage is so moving that it's read at many weddings and funerals.

Many wonder what God requires of us. The prophet Micah spells it out very clearly, "What does the Lord require of you? To do justice, love kindness, and walk humbly with God." (Micah 6:8).

As you read the Bible and talk with others, you will find passages that ring with divine truth for you. The ongoing challenge of following Jesus is to allow these passages to shape our daily actions and our view of humanity in general. When I work to apply the Bible, it fills me with humility.

Each time I work to apply the Bible to my life, I remind myself that blood was shed because of these pages. Wars were fought over what people thought God revealed through these pages. Soldiers packed a Bible with them as a necessary part of their armor. Patients have a Bible beside them in pre-op rooms as they await life-threatening surgery. Prisoners have a Bible with them in their jail cells.

A follower of Jesus I knew committed a serious mistake. But it was more than a mistake; it was a crime, it was something terrible. During the trial, he kept his Bible beside him, not because he was righteous, but because it reminded him of how wrong he was, how he needed to repent, and how God was with him during these hard times. After he was found guilty and sentenced, he was led away in shackles. They let him keep one thing, his Bible. I'll never forget my last image of him, his wrists handcuffed, his legs in chains, his Bible tucked under his arm.

These images and memories keep me humble when applying the Bible. Some followers of Jesus feel self-righteous when they interpret and apply the Bible. They swing the Bible like a bat against other people. They know they are God's special messengers in revealing God's truth. They miss or ignore the passages where Jesus taught about being meek (Matthew 5:5), and about hungering and thirsting for righteousness (Matthew 5:6). They miss Jesus's teaching that the greatest is the lowest and the servant of all (Matthew 18:4). They forget to apply Paul's teaching that in the name of Jesus every knee shall bow (Philippians 2:10).

Reading the Bible drives us to our knees. The more I study, earn academic degrees, and read books, I'm humbled and reminded of how much I still have to learn and to know that thousands of authors before me have guided followers of Jesus through the scriptures for centuries.

We need to be humble as we contemplate God's revelation, inspiration, and personal application. No one has ever mastered the entire mystery of the scriptures. In the past, God revealed divine truth through the scriptures, and God continues to speak through the scriptures today.

There are as many interpretations and applications of the Bible as there are those whose hearts are opened to its pages.

When we follow the Jesus Path, we need to allow room for God to speak, move, convict, and lead individual hearts as God did with those first followers of Jesus. A humble teacher knows how to get out of God's way and allow God to interact with someone directly. A humble student sometimes goes beyond what a teacher says the Bible might mean and interprets the text for themselves. A humble person knows when they need others to help them interpret the Bible. Even though I've studied the Bible for years, I still seek counsel from friends and scholars about what certain passages may mean. As we apply the message with humility, it brings wisdom.

Wisdom

I pray for wisdom each time I read the Bible. I need wisdom because the Bible can be difficult and complicated to read.

I try to be a faithful follower of Jesus. I love my wife. I love my children. I love my parents and siblings. Jesus said, "Whoever comes to me and does not hate father, mother, wife, and children, brothers and sisters, yes, even life itself cannot be my disciple" (Luke 14:26). A passage like this makes me nauseous. Is Jesus really asking me to hate my family to be his disciple? I don't think so. I need the wisdom to interpret and apply this passage considering Jesus's teaching of love.

I have a home. I want to shelter my family. I have toys and possessions. My garage is full of cars, sporting equipment, and stuff I can't bear to throw away. I'm a North American Christian living in the wealthiest society in the history of the world. And when I read Jesus say, "None of you can become my disciple if you do not give up all your possessions," (Luke 14:33). This passage makes me twitch. I know I will never sell all my possessions. The guy who said, "God said it, I believe it, that's it" cherished his wife and kids. He owns a sprawling home and several cars. God said it, he believed it, and he still lives contrary to what Jesus taught. Does this mean that we are not faithful? Does this mean we don't want to follow Jesus? I don't think so. However, it does challenge us to use wisdom as we apply passages like this to our lives. These scriptures hold us accountable to live simply by remembering the vast number of people in the world live in poverty. It challenges us to live in such a way that we are not over consuming the world's resources.

I could go on and on. Even the most devout follower of Jesus falls short of his teachings. Our lives contradict what we profess to believe. Therefore, when we strive to apply the scripture to our lives, we need to go beyond the legalist codes of behavior.

Jesus hated legalism and legalists. While he believed in the law of God (Matthew 5:18), he hated the legal codes binding people in ethical chains. He despised the Scribes and Pharisees who authored these codes of behavior. The entire twenty-third chapter of Matthew is a harsh critique of these Scribes and Pharisees. Jesus called them, "Blind guides, snakes, broods of vipers." What angered Jesus was that they "tied up heavy burdens and laid them on the shoulders of others (23:5). He said to the Scribes and Pharisees, ". . .you have neglected the weightier matters of the law, justice and mercy, and faith" (23:23). Jesus said their concern with legalism was like, "Straining a gnat but swallowing a camel." The Scribes and Pharisees completely missed Jesus's message. Jesus didn't want legalism, he wanted people's hearts (Matthew 9:13). If I gave you a concrete list of behaviors that you must apply to your life based on what I believe the scriptures taught, and then gave you a legal code, I'm no better than a Scribe or Pharisee. A legal code doesn't save you, your relationship with Jesus does. To apply the Bible, our relationship with

Jesus should be formed by our personal interaction with it and a community of others we have joined. This is why the Path of Community is so crucial.

As we engage in personal prayer, meditation, contemplation, and journaling—the Path of Prayer and devotion, God convicts our hearts on what needs to change in our lives. Just sit down and start reading the Sermon on the Mount (Matthew 5, 6, and 7) you will feel the divine baker kneading your heart and punching down the dough of your soul.

Another way of learning how to apply the teachings of Jesus is to sit with groups of other followers of Jesus and talk about how they interpret scripture. Remember, the Spirit of Jesus is present in groups. God convicts people's hearts when they are in groups where someone is trained in the gift of interpretation. There are times when you feel God speaking directly to you as someone shares their interpretation of scripture. This is why we can't be followers of Jesus on our own. The Path of Community teaches us this later in this book. We need others to teach us how to apply the messages of the Bible.

God inspires your heart as you seek to apply the scriptures. There will be times where the scriptures make your heart sing because you are fulfilling what Jesus desires from you. And there will be times when you are on your knees asking for God's forgiveness. There will be moments where you know you are missing the mark and you know you need to change.

When you engage in daily devotions and group study you might have to bite your tongue because of what you want to say to someone, but you won't because the scripture rings in your head, ". . .and they kept their silence" (Acts 15:12). There will be times when your heart is like putty when you're with someone who's hurting. You hold them like a child because you read where Jesus said, "Suffer the little children to come to me" (Matthew 19:14). You embrace them and are the living Christ for them. This is how someone in a relationship with Jesus lives rather than with a legal code. As you live with Jesus, as you follow his paths, he teaches you how to respond. This is what it means to be faithful.

Authority

God revealed the truth, authors are inspired to write, you work to interpret and apply the scriptures, so how do you make them authoritative? Let's look at the authority of the Bible.

Some followers of Jesus argue that the Bible's authority does not depend on the person or group studying it. The Bible's authority exists independent of any person. These followers argue that since God revealed the Bible, it is innately authoritative. They believe in the complete and total acceptance of the Bible as it is written. However, do these people have Bibles sitting on their shelves gathering dust? If you don't read, interpret, and apply it to your life, then there is very little authority over you. The Bible has authority in our lives when we make it authoritative. We need to measure our thoughts and behaviors with these teachings and allow them to convict and change us. If we're angry, frustrated, or bitter, then Jesus's two great commandments need to be authoritative, and we need to change. If we're judging people, we need to listen to Jesus say, "Do not judge and you will not be judged" (Luke 6:37). If we find we're holding grudges against someone who wronged us, then we need to heed Jesus's teaching, "Forgive and you will be forgiven" (Luke 6:37). We need to let go of the bile and anger and grant forgiveness. When we conform our lives to the teachings of the Bible where God revealed the truth, then we make the Bible authoritative.

Kissing the Text

We have done a lot of work studying the Bible, reading and applying it to our lives. It can be demanding to read the Bible. As followers of Jesus, we need to shift gears from studying the Bible to allowing the Bible to study us. Let me share with you how I do this.

Grab your Bible, not the e-Bible, but the one with the leather cover and pages that you can turn. Pick it up and look at it. Look at the binding. Is it cracked from years of use or so new you can smell the glue from the factory? Feel the heft of the Bible in your hand. Is it heavy like a burden or light like a blessing? Are your pages dog-eared from years of thumbing through it? Is it brand new or passed down generation to generation? This is *your* Bible, a gift from God to you.

Now, open this gift and prepare to hear God speak to you. Sometimes it feels like a stirring in your gut, a pounding in your heart, or a whirl of ideas in your head. You may even hear God speak in a clear, still voice. Get ready; it will happen.

I have heard God speak to me when using a form of reading called *Lectio Divina*, Latin for, "Sacred Reading." Followers of Jesus have used *Lectio Divina* allowing God to speak to them for over a thousand years.

You can do *Lectio* with any passage of the Bible. I prefer to use a devotional guide which gives me a daily passage. You can download several devotional books or purchase different Apps. I turn to the passage for the day and take a few minutes to be still. I breathe and quiet myself. I come to the passage expecting that God will speak to me and reveal truth. I read the passage very slowly. Sometimes I read it out loud. When I'm done, I bend my head down, raise the Bible to my lips, and I kiss the pages of the Bible.

I know, it sounds strange. When I first read the Bible this way and kissed the pages, I looked around to see if anybody was watching. I felt embarrassed. Over the years I've become accustomed to kissing the pages of the Bible. I kiss it as I would kiss the head of a child. I kiss it as something tender, special, or sacred. Kissing the Bible reminds me of all the millions of people who picked this book up before me. Kissing the Bible reminds me to be humble, gentle, and holy.

I read the passage at least three times and sometimes as often as twenty. I allow ample time, sometimes as much as several hours, other times as few as fifteen minutes. I wait for the passage to settle into me. I absorb the words like a dry sponge. Slowly I wait for a word, a phrase, a sentence, a paragraph to move me. There are times when nothing happens, and it's good enough just to be quiet with the Bible. Other times though, I feel God speak to me through the passage. Sometimes a word addresses an issue I've been facing. Other times the passage challenges me to change.

I keep a journal beside me to note the words or sentences that move me. I write down what I feel God is saying to me. I end each time by praying for humility and wisdom.

At odd moments throughout the day—at stoplights, doing the dishes, or walking across a parking lot—I find myself thinking about the passage. The verses massage my heart all day long. They take on a unique authority as I seek to embody the teachings in my personal behavior. Day in and day out, God leads me through *Lectio Divina*.

From the Ashes Comes a Blessing

The day I burned my Bible I told myself I would never read this book again. It was just too painful. It wasn't until someone told me to stop taking the Bible literally, to go beyond legalisms, to not swing it like a bat at my soul and allow it to be a blessing.

The Bible became a blessing when I read Paul's writing on love, "faith, hope, and love, these three abide, but the greatest of these is love" (1 Corinthians 13:13). I remembered Jesus teaching that his purpose for coming was to bring a full sense of joy to my life. The Bible taught me that God doesn't abandon us. It wasn't long before I picked up the Bible again. I started reading. I was taught how to kiss the pages. I felt God speaking directly to my soul. I loved to feel the Bible in my hands. When I saw people I knew and love reading the Bible, it gave me the courage to return to its pages. Slowly over the years I began to realize that this amazing book was indeed a great blessing.

Chapter Five: The Path of God's Will

I'm not at my best when someone tells me to do something. I'm a strong-willed person. Some may even say I'm stubborn. I've never outgrown the rebellious teenager stage. If someone tells me I can't do something, usually I am inclined to go the other way. I want to choose for myself.

I've always wrestled with this. I want to do what I want to do, yet God invites me to set aside my will and choose God's Will instead. I must work at, and at times struggle to figure out what God wants me to do. Then I must take the next step and choose for God's desire.

As much as I struggle with God's Will, I believe it's one of the essential paths we follow. As followers of Jesus, we are invited to use the gift of our free will and choose to fulfill God's Will. People who can do this inspire me. When I think about those who were able to choose God's Will, I think of John.

When do you take a loved one off a life support system? It's one of the most challenging decisions a family makes. I stood with John at the bedside of his wife in intensive care. She had suffered a major stroke and was on a ventilator. The doctors told him she wouldn't survive if removed from life support, but they couldn't decide for him. John had to do what was best—he had to choose. Did he keep her ventilated hoping she would somehow recover, or choose to remove her? As I stood with John, he asked me, "Steve, what do you think I should do? What do you think God's Will is?"

While John had a choice, he wanted to choose God's Will. We talked about his feelings on living, and the meaning of the quality of life.

Was the doctor's diagnosis correct? We talked about the scripture's teaching of love and compassion. John wanted to take twenty-four hours to think and pray about it. The next day John and I met again at his wife's bedside. He said, "Steve, after praying about this I believe it is God's Will to remove her from life support." When the doctors removed the ventilator, it took twenty-six hours for her to pass away. During those hours John wrestled with his decision; did he make the right choice? Slowly, hour-by-hour, John's wife slipped from life, entering into the resurrection.

John inspires me because while he wanted to *will* his wife to live, as one who is following Jesus at this critical moment of his life, he wanted to pursue something greater for his life—God's Will.

Think about your life right now. It could be that you are also at a junction. Your life could go in one of two directions, if not multiple directions. Perhaps you have a career opportunity. Maybe you're contemplating which school to attend. Or maybe you are facing an ethical dilemma. When you stand at these crossroads there is a myriad of options, but which one reflects God's Will for your life?

God's Will; it's an interesting term. God gave us free will, yet there is another presence in our lives which reflects a greater desire, a greater hope, and a greater dream. It's God's Will. Followers of Jesus are invited when they make decisions in life to discern the divine will for their lives and choose this instead.

Jesus and God's Will

Jesus shared two central teachings about God's Will. When he taught the disciples how to pray the Lord's prayer, he said, "Thy kingdom come; *thy will* be done on earth as it is in heaven" (Matthew

6:10). In this phrase, Jesus taught that there was a divine desire, a divine intention, and a divine will guiding all that is done in the heavens. He taught us to pray that this same intention will also hold sway on earth.

Jesus modeled the second teaching when he was in the Garden of Gethsemane. The night before he was arrested, he prayed, "My father, if it is possible, let this cup pass from me, yet not what I want but what you want" (Matthew 26:39). Jesus presents that there are two desires in his life: there is what he wants, and then there is what God wants. He doesn't want to be arrested, and he recognizes he has a choice. He could get up, take the disciples, and leave. But he also realizes there is a divine bias for the situation.

Two verses later Jesus prays, "My Father if this cannot pass unless I drink it, your will be done" (Matthew 26:42). Jesus models that he has discerned God's Will and is ready to surrender himself to fulfill this divine desire. He sets aside what he wants so God's greater purpose can be fulfilled. Jesus presents the example we are to follow when called to make choices in our life.

Discerning God's Will

My stubborn nature put me at odds with God's Will. I can teach what the Bible says, and I know Jesus's teaching, yet I have my will and opinions I want to pursue. Yet, as a follower of Jesus, my greater desire is to live as Jesus lived. If Jesus was able to set aside his will, then that's my desire as well. My challenge then is how do I discern God's Will? If John can do this, then how do I learn to do the same? I found three central passages from the Bible acting as a compass leading us to God's Will.

God's Will always coincides with the two great commandments taught by Jesus, "Love the Lord your God with all of your heart, soul, mind, and strength and love your neighbor as yourself" (Matthew 22:34-40). The embodiment of God's Will is in love; a love for God, a love for self, and a love for neighbors.

A second teaching is in Micah 6:8, "What does the Lord require of us, but to do justice, love kindness, and walk humbly with our Lord." Micah describes God's Will as containing justice, working to live in such a way that all of God's children have equal access to the goods, bounty, plenty, rights, freedoms, and privileges of every other child of God.

God's Will contains kindness and compassion. Therefore, one of the core paths is compassion and service. Choosing to live with compassion brings God's Will to fruition.

God's Will embodies humility. It reflects our desire to get out of God's way. It's checking our ego at the door. It's the desire to work for the greater good.

The third Bible passage is Jeremiah 29:11 "For surely I know the plans I have for you, plans for your welfare and not for harm, to give you a future with hope." There are some key words in this passage. God has "plans for us." Instead of one clear choice, God's Will encompasses *plans,* options, choices, and multiple paths. Each of God's plans includes welfare, "not to harm us" . . . God's Will is never self-destructive. God's Will may require sacrifice, but never self-abuse. God's Will embodies a hopeful future. When we contemplate God's Will for our lives, it always brings hopefulness.

These three verses: the two great commandments; the requirements of the Lord; and God's plans for our lives; serve as the North Star guiding our actions. These verses provide the curbs on our road keeping us traveling down the right path.

Consider John's story. John's decision reflected God's Will. He based his decision on love. He loved his wife and wanted the best for her. However, he also realized that there was no hope for a meaningful quality of life. Her hope was not in this life, but the hope of resurrection. He had to humbly set aside his desire that she might have a life with him, and instead bow before God's greater purpose.

Hard Decisions

John learned that God's Will is often the hard choice. Sometimes there are multiple options, each full of God's love. The choices can be paralyzing as we realize each one has a different life path. The challenge here is to choose! Make a choice, begin to act, we need to hear God say to us, "Don't be afraid to choose! Exercise your will!" God is waiting for us to decide. Too often people waffle on making that choice. Consider Tom's story.

Tom found himself at a crossroads. He was in a satisfying sales job. He was financially successful, able to pay his bills, as well as build up a large savings account. Yet, Tom was frustrated with his life. His heart just wasn't in his job. Tom felt his passion lay in writing. He wanted to quit his job and take the risk of writing full time. But it was a hard choice; he would leave financial security for financial uncertainty. Tom found himself on the fence and struggled with this choice for years. All along God was saying to Tom, "Not my will but thy will be done." God works with Tom no matter what his decision is. There's no judgment on God's part. God is active in Tom's life regardless of his decision. However, for years God was waiting for Tom to choose.

When Life Implodes

Discerning God's Will for our lives takes on more significance when our lives seem to be imploding. Maybe we made bad decisions, or we have been the victim of someone's evil choices, or we've been diagnosed with an illness or a disease. Where is God's Will in all this? Where is the divine bias and dream when our world falls in? At this point, I believe it's important to understand the deeper aspect of God's Will. Instead of something we choose, God's Will is a force that works on our behalf.

Leslie Weatherhead in his book, *The Will of God* describes the three phases of the Will of God: an intentional will, a circumstantial will, and an ultimate will. Weatherhead says these three phases of God's Will is like a stream flowing down the side of a mountain.

The intentional Will of God is the stream starting at the top of a mountain. God intends the stream to flow down the mountainside and join the river in the valley below. However, the stream encounters different types of obstacles and circumstances, impeding the flow of the stream. There are rocks, boulders, and fallen trees that may even dam the stream. But the stream has an inherent force, a pressure, and a will pushing against the circumstances that have fallen into the stream. Eventually, the will of the stream overcomes the obstacles and continues to flow down the mountainside. The ultimate Will of God is when the stream joins the river on the valley floor. The stream's original intention is realized. The obstacles are overcome, and the fullness of the stream is embodied. The *will of the stream* carried it down the hillside.

Imagine your life is the stream. God's Will is embedded in you and is a force moving through you. Like the stream, God has an intentional will for you. These intentions are that you are rich with bounty and blessing, you are full of satisfaction, you enjoy the riches and the fullness of life, and you have health, wholeness, and well-being.

However, as you live, and the stream of your life flows down the mountain side, you encounter different circumstances that begin damming the stream. You're laid off from work, your spouse develops cancer, or your parents are killed in a car wreck. Accidents and tragedies occur to the point where you feel that God has abandoned you. Yet, the Will of God, like the force in the stream, pushes and pushes. God's Will works to bring a sense of hope and optimism. The Will of God pushes through the obstacles. The challenge is if God is with you, can you be with God?

It's a great challenge. When the world crashes in on us, we're tempted to feel abandoned by God. If so, then we can and should walk away from God. Instead, we need to hang in there with God. We need to be patient as God finds a new way. We need to do all in our power to work with God. We need to keep working and being proactive in our challenges. We need to apply for jobs, seek counseling, and get second opinions from doctors. We need to stay connected with God through prayer, scripture reading, and involvement in a faith community. Followers of Jesus continue to work during challenging times. They do not give up, nor do they give in. You need to bring as much energy and creativity possible when dealing with your circumstances.

God's Will promises ultimately the force of God overcomes the obstacles damming the stream of your life. Eventually God brings you to a new day, a new stage of your life. Mike is someone who embodies the stream of God's Will.

Mike, diagnosed with stage four prostate cancer, was told to go home and enjoy the last six months of his life. A giant just tree fell across the stream of his life. However, Mike refused to give up. He believed it wasn't God's Will for him to die yet and that God was going to work in and through him. Because of Mike's cancer, he felt more connected to God than he ever had. He spent more time in prayer, attended church, and connected with his community. He also began to look for other options to deal with his cancer. He got second and third opinions. He signed up for drug trials and stayed committed to a healthy lifestyle. Three years later Mike is still alive. God's Will is working through his cancer.

However, what if Mike was not cured? What if Mike eventually dies from cancer? Where is God's Will then? It's here that we need to understand the ultimate Will of God for Mike and all of us.

God's ultimate Will is for us to be united with God. This unity only happens after our death. Just because Mike dies doesn't mean God's Will ends. We enter into the resurrection after death, which we'll discuss in the concluding path of the book. We need to realize that death is not a tragedy for God; it's merely a transition. God's Will overcomes death, the greatest obstacle we face. It ushers us into complete and total unity with God. God's Will works while Mike lives, and God's Will is ultimately realized if, and when, Mike dies.

Empowering Others

There are times when my stubborn way is an asset for God's Will. While it may be difficult to choose God's Will for myself, I'm deeply committed to empowering others to discover God's Will for themselves. I believe in fulfilling Micah's statement to "do justice."

Many people in the world live in oppression and poverty. The circumstances of their lives have dammed the stream of God's Will. The force of God's Will is working to change their conditions, but for this to happen, God needs us to act on their behalf. Justice is when we sacrifice ourselves for the benefit of others so that God's Will is realized.

Each of the Jesus Paths is utilized when we embody Micah's justice. We pray for those under the thumb of oppression. We study the scriptures to understand how God expects us to act on behalf of those who are suffering. We dig deep into the issues to understand the evil acts driving oppression. We work to understand the complex systems causing poverty and oppression. We use our lives to bring about change and this often requires a stubborn attitude. People in power don't like it when they're confronted with their destructive actions. Systems that oppress people reject those who seek to change them. As people who follow Jesus, we take a stubborn attitude and do not back down, play small, or give up.

When we dive deep into the complex issues, we often discover there are institutions, businesses, and individuals who benefit from oppression and poverty. As we learn about these issues, the call to fulfill God's Will drives us to speak the truth of the injustices. The followers of the Jesus Path are led to participate in social issues. We commit ourselves to the rights of race, gender, and sexual orientation. We take unpopular stands when we realize those who are causing poverty and oppression are thwarting God's Will. Committing ourselves to justice fulfills Jesus's two great commandments. It is out of our love for God that we work on behalf of others. Jeremiah's call to an abundant life drives us to work so that all will celebrate the blessings that God has for us.

Commitment

Those who intentionally choose to live the Jesus Path commit themselves to God's Will. We know that God's Will is a force in our lives as we seek its guidance and direction. As we make decisions, we ask ourselves which option fulfills the two great commandments. We ponder how our actions allow us to follow Micah's guidance to do justice, love kindness, and walk humbly with God. Following Jeremiah's insight, we ask ourselves which choice enables us to have an abundant life? We act on choices that best fulfill these standards.

When we face calamity on the Jesus Path, or when the circumstances of life crash around us, we grieve and feel frustrated, but we do not give up hope. We do not give up on God. We know that God's Will is active and pushing against our circumstances. We know God will bring us to a new day, even if that new day is resurrection following death.

Following God's Will brings tremendous joy for those of us on the Jesus Path. We realize we are God's presence in the world. God's dream is fulfilled in our lives and in the lives of others as we seek to love God, ourselves, and others.

I still find it difficult to set aside my will and choose for God. It's easy to teach and hard to live. I still want to do things my way. Sometimes I realize this is precisely what God wants me to do. God needs me to choose and live. God has a dream for my life and it is only realized if I get off my backside and engage the world.

There are other times though when I feel an itch of sorts, a discomfort, a nagging sense that I'm called to do something else. I feel God calling me to set aside my stubborn will and work to discern something different. For me, this is hard work. I need to remind myself to follow Jesus's teaching and say, "Not my will, but thy will be done." I must measure myself against the teachings of Jesus, Micah, and Jeremiah. After reflecting and ruminating on these passages, I often seek out the counsel of those in my community. When I discover what God wants me to do, what God's Will is for a particular situation, I have to stubbornly choose to act on God's behalf. While this doesn't always take me down a path I would choose, I've found peace knowing it is God's desire.

There have also been times when my life has imploded. I've made bad choices, one of my children had a life-threatening illness, and I spent a night in jail when someone stole my identity and committed a crime in my name. It's during these times when I've had to be stubborn. I could not give up. I had to believe God's Will was working on my behalf overcoming these obstacles bringing me to a place of peace and happiness. It's taken months, even years to realize God's ultimate Will for my life, but in each circumstance, I've experienced God's dream.

My greatest challenge still lies before me, my death. It's here where I'm invited to practice everything I've taught. At that moment, I pray that I'll set my stubborn nature aside and accept God's ultimate Will for my life, to enter into resurrection and be fully united with God.

John, Tom, and Mike are average people. They're not great heroes or pillars of faith. They were living their life and faced with complex circumstances. Yet, they modeled the challenge each of us face who walk the Jesus path. As we live, we aspire to do what Jesus did and respond to God by saying, "Not my will, but your will be done."

Chapter Six: The Path of Community

It's Christmas Eve. The church is packed with those who only come on this one sacred night. For me, it's the holiest night of the church year. Followers of Jesus from around the world gather to celebrate his birth. Christmas Eve transcends nationalities, politics, or social agendas. On this beautiful night, we forget that the church is splintered into thirty-three thousand different denominations—instead we are one body of Christ.

On this night, we read scriptures, sing carols, and listen to music. In some churches, children reenact the Christmas story in a pageant of fun, and often chaos. Sometimes we celebrate Jesus's last supper. We eat bread and drink wine or juice.

Something magical happens at the finale of the worship service. As people enter the sanctuary, they are given a small candle. They hold onto this candle anticipating what's to come at the end of the service. Then the sanctuary is darkened. I light a small candle, raise it high, and talk about being the light of Christ in the world. While singing the carol, *Silent Night*, I walk down the center lighting the candles of those on each side of the aisle. They then turn and light the candle of the one beside them. One by one the entire sanctuary fills with candlelight. As *Silent Night* ends we raise our candles and look around at the beautiful lights casting a golden glow throughout the church. I end the service by quoting a passage from the Gospel of John, "The light shines in the darkness and the darkness has not overcome it." The glow of the candles represents what it means to be part of a church community. During our pain and despair, members of the church are the lights shining in the darkness. Our lives are filled with the joy of following Jesus, and we then share his love with our church community. We depart this sacred night, dedicating ourselves to be the light of Jesus. The great Christmas Carol, *Joy to the World*, wraps up the feeling of Christmas Eve—Jesus is our joy. It's all about joy.

Joy!

When we participate in a community that follows Jesus, it is pure joy.

In the same way that I love the Bible, am dedicated to prayer, and seek to follow God's Will, I also celebrate being part of a community who follows Jesus. Every Sunday as we gather to celebrate and worship together, I can't wait to visit with those who traveled through the week. But it's just not on Sunday. People gather in communities of faith throughout the week to worship and learn together. The key is to "gather together."

I tried following Jesus on my own, but it doesn't work. I miss the joy of participating in a community. I make mistakes when I follow Jesus on my own. I choose the Bible passages I agree with to follow and ignore the passages I don't like. I am sure my pet peeves are the same as Jesus's issues as well. Before I know it, I try to make Jesus follow me instead of me following Jesus. This doesn't mean I don't like being on my own with Jesus. The Path of Prayer is very clear on how significant it is to meditate and pray alone with God. However, I've learned that it's more than just me; it's me and every other follower of Jesus.

The Parade

To follow Jesus is like joining a parade, participating in a movement, or melding into a huge amoeba spreading and changing as it moves through people's lives. You may not know where the amoeba is moving; you're just part of the whole. You become swept up in its energy, excitement, and enthusiasm. The spirit of Jesus moves, shapes, and inspires. Followers of Jesus are reminded that when they come together they are not alone, he is with them. It's one of his basic teachings, "Wherever two or more are gathered in my name, there I am also" (Matthew 18:20). Following Jesus means leaving yourself behind, losing yourself, and joining with others on the way.

The Way

The first followers of Jesus called themselves, "People of the Way," or just, "The Way." They felt that following Jesus was a way of life. They also referred to themselves as "The Called-Out Ones." They believed they were called out of their normal lives, their everyday existence, as well as their homes and businesses. They joined together to create God's kingdom on earth. The Greek word for "The Called-Out Ones" when translated into English is "Church." Today when we think of "church," we tend to think of properties and buildings. The first followers of Jesus saw themselves in a completely different way. "Church" meant a group of people scattered and gathered. The first churches met in homes, business, fields, town centers, at the edges of rivers; any place they could gather. They talked, sang, and prayed. Their scriptures were the Hebrew Bible. Letters from Paul and other letters written by emerging church leaders slowly made their way through the different communities where they were read and shared. As the gospels were written, they too were shared and read. At their meetings people brought food; it was a potluck, a party. They loved being together; they felt joy. At times it was hard and complicated, but the people of The Church, the Called-Out Ones, found strength and courage when persecuted by the Roman Empire. They found solace in each other's company, and they comforted each other in grief. They felt something holy when they gathered; they felt the presence of Jesus.

The Body of Christ

People flocked to The Way. The more these early followers of Jesus were persecuted by the Roman Empire, the more others joined them. These communities grew in numbers. They went from being a movement to organizing communities in Italy, Greece, and Turkey. The rapid growth was exciting, but it also became a challenge. Some of the joy was lost as they argued over who should lead, speak, and teach. The arguments became so intense that Paul needed to address the conflict. It prompted him to write letters to the Church at Corinth, what is now known as first and second Corinthians in the Bible.

During this conflict, Paul gave a lasting image of what it means to participate in a church. He described the church as the body of Christ (1 Corinthians 12:12-31). Just as Christ was a living body while he walked the earth, the members of the church were now the living spiritual body of Christ. These communities were the head, hands, arms, and feet of Christ. They should model themselves as Christ's living body. Some would be the head, others the eyes, and others the hands. Just as in a real body the head cannot say to the hand, I don't have any need of you, so in Christ's body, it is the same (I Corinthians 12:12-21). Paul's vision treated all as equals. This included everyone. No one was left out.

Above all, Paul wanted them to see the one powerful image that would hold them together; it was love. The church's purpose was to love and serve one another. Paul's chapter on church structure is considered one of the greatest chapters in the Bible. It's commonly known as "The Love Chapter" (1 Corinthians 13). "Love is patient, kind, not envious, boastful, arrogant, or rude. It does not insist on its own way; it is not irritable or resentful; it doesn't rejoice in wrongdoing but rejoices in the truth. It bears all things, believes all things, hopes all things, and endures all things" (vs. 4-7).

This passage is frequently read at weddings. While it's a beautiful description of two people in a relationship, it's really about how members of the church are to treat one another.

I imagine as the church read Paul's letters to the Corinthians, they began to realize they were the lights shining in the darkness. They were more than just a church organization; they loved each other. They had hope amid the Roman oppression. They were changing the way people saw God.

Changing the Way People See God

Peasants had difficult lives in the Roman Empire. They were often outcasts in communities and cultures. They scraped together a living through hard labor and a meager diet. Death was predominant. For every live birth, a woman gave birth to eight babies. When the church reached out to those on the fringes of society, peasants saw a God who cared about their plight.

The vision of the churches also inspired wealthy people. They saw a model that treated everyone as equals. While they could follow several Gods within the Empire, the vision of God led by Jesus was the one that attracted them.

Both the peasants and the wealthy joined the churches, attracted by the vision of love embodied by the members. The Gods of the Empire demanded sacrifice, the God of the churches required love. The way participants lived changed the way people saw God. It was through their actions that the path of Jesus began to spread.

Lights, Love, and Change

Today our faith communities are led by this same vision. Just as the early church was structured around love, so are we. We are to be points of light amid people's suffering. Our vision of the body of Christ reaches those suffering along the edges of poverty as well as the wealthy in urban and suburban communities. Following Jesus creates a new vision.

People in our culture often view followers of Jesus as judgmental, angry, and exclusive. When this is the case, they project these same images on God, and God appears judgmental, angry, and exclusive as well. We change the way people see God only through the actions of the church. Through our communities, God's love shines through us. We show a God who is with those amid the circumstances of their life, especially their pain and sorrow.

No One Cries Alone

One of my first teachers taught that following Jesus meant no one had to cry alone. I love that. It gets at the heart of what it means to follow him. Let's face it; life is brutal, it beats you up. The harder life becomes, the more alone you feel, especially when the tears come. Have you ever had something break your soul; that leaves you crying to the point where you wonder where all the water comes from to make those tears? It's during this type of pain when a follower of Jesus comes with love and compassion and sits with you, sharing your burden.

A member of the church is like Simon of Cyrene. Simon helped carry Jesus's cross. Jesus, whipped by the Roman guards, was forced to carry his cross to the place of crucifixion. Jesus was beaten so badly he tripped several times, falling to the ground. A Roman guard grabbed a man from the crowd to help Jesus carry his cross. This man was Simon of Cyrene (Matthew 27:32).

Simon got underneath the cross and helped Jesus carry his burden. This is what people do who are part of a community that follows Jesus. When people are beaten and broken by life, others help carry their burdens. Out of this desire, communities build homes, schools, and hospitals. They are points of light, people of love, and they change the way people see God. But wiping away the tears is the real heavy lifting done by the followers of Jesus.

The 911 attacks left people stunned throughout the United States. The evening of 911, communities of faith became a gathering place. At our church, we opened the doors and people flooded in. The sanctuary was full of those in tears. We sang songs, prayed, lit candles, and sat in silence. One of our youth read the poem of St. Francis, "Make me an instrument of peace" The gathering in this place touched the depths of what it means for us to follow Jesus, to be instruments of peace instead of war. But the most important thing we did was hold each other. It's what followers of Jesus do. As we sat and cried and prayed, we all felt something. We knew we were not alone. He was with us.

The same is true for the pain people face in life; death, job loss, crippling diseases, depression, or mental illness. The community of faith reaches out to them. They listen to their sorrow and confusion. They embody what Paul taught: love. Followers of Jesus are loving people. They change the way people see God. God is not a distant deity; instead, the followers of Jesus show people that God is close, intimate, and personal.

Dirty Laundry

I've often wonder why something so wonderful, moving, and profound is so hard. Those who fight the hardest are usually the people who claim to love Jesus the most. Over my years as a pastor, I've seen followers of Jesus fight over the stupidest things: who gets to hang things on the church walls? What kind of music is played? Who gives money and who doesn't? Did the preacher really say that (which in my instance is usually a legit complaint)? But it's often petty stuff. Is this why Paul had to preach about love to his churches—they forgot about it, just like we have? I was once embroiled in an ugly fight between churches. It was so bad we had to bring in an outside consultant.

Our consultant, Walter Bruggeman, is a biblical scholar of great renown. We hoped he could help us find a way to resolve our conflict. Walter looked long and hard at all the ministers of the churches. He then said, "church fights are so bitter because there's so little to lose." We squirmed.

Walter was right. It was little. It was stupid. Yet it still took years to resolve. Many people left our churches because of the conflict. We had to wait for a few people to die before the conflict was fully resolved. They took the conflict to their graves and nearly took our churches with them. This is how bad conflict can be and how ugly followers of Jesus can get.

Those who follow Jesus are still human. They're messy; they have histories, feelings, and emotions. They have shadows they haven't managed very well. Some people have so little control over what happens in their lives that they want one place that doesn't change. So, they want to put their community in a historical lockbox. These people wreak a great deal of havoc and a lot of pain. To be honest, there are times I wish those people would leave the church. They bring out the worst in me and I grow weary of their complaining. I curse them under my breath; hence this is why I need to manage my own shadow.

But if these difficult people leave the community of Jesus, then I'd have to leave as well because Jesus said, "He who is without sin cast the first stone," (John 8:7). Granted, I've had a stone in my hand, my arm was cocked, and I knew if the Lord wasn't looking I would have hurled away. What's stopped me is that I can feel Jesus staring at me with a raised eyebrow thinking, "Go ahead Mr. Pure. Cast the first stone." I'm suddenly reminded of all my mistakes, faults, imperfections, and the number of times I've missed the mark. As I hold that stone, I suddenly see the faces of all those who've been patient with me. So, I've learned to drop the stone and get better at dealing with conflict. It's what you must do if you're going to follow Jesus and be a part of a community. You must get good at dealing with conflict.

Just the word, "conflict" makes people queasy. But it's part of life, even the Christian life. One of my teachers once said, "Conflict isn't unchristian, it's how Christians deal with conflict that makes it unchristian."

A story in the book of Acts describes the first great church fight. The church leaders had a debate about how Paul and Barnabas were converting all the Gentiles to follow Jesus. In the middle of the debate Luke said, "They all kept silent and listened" (Acts 15:12). I've found that that one sentence solves most church fights—they kept silent and listened.

To keep silent and listen requires humility, which leads to wisdom, and wisdom leads to inspiration. It's the same for the Path of Scripture. Humility and wisdom are two of the main tenets to following Jesus. Whether it's a church of ten thousand meeting in a sports arena, or a church of thirty meeting in a living room, you have to be humble and remind yourself that it's not about you. It's about Jesus. If you're going to hear Jesus, you need to be willing to be silent and listen. You're going to have to go out of your way, get underneath someone's cross and carry it. It takes work to see the world through someone else's eyes. You may have to surrender what you feel is valuable, important, and maybe even sacred, so that all might follow Jesus.

Going back to the first great church fight from Acts, Peter and the church in Jerusalem had to completely let go of circumcision, one of their most sacred beliefs. Paul and Barnabus knew circumcision was a showstopper for Gentiles. Imagine Paul sharing the love of Jesus, the gift of grace, and people respond by giving their life to follow the Jesus Path. Then Paul must tell the men, "By the way, there's something we didn't tell you . . ."

What if Peter and the Church in Jerusalem had insisted on maintaining the rite of circumcision? What if they felt it was too sacred and was paramount to be a follower of Jesus? The church would have stayed a little Jewish sect, and it would have died. But because they were willing to keep silent and listen, they let go, and the church took off like a sprinter from the blocks. It makes me wonder what God could do if the rest of us let go of our petty complaints.

When followers of Jesus get roiled in a conflict, they need to remember he had a wide-open view of what it meant to follow him. One time some of Jesus's disciples were upset and angry that others were preaching and casting out demons in Jesus's name. They asked Jesus if they should be stopped because they didn't have the proper authority. Jesus said, "Don't stop them. If they're not against us, they're for us" (Mark 9:38-41). I think most followers of Jesus get this backward. They think, if they're not following Jesus our way, then they're wrong, and they're against us. Jesus knew there would be different understandings of what it meant to follow him. As followers of Jesus, we must allow ample room for people to express their faith. Would this heal the rifts between the thirty-three thousand different denominations? What if we allowed room for each of us to express our faith and all be a part of Christ's great church? Wouldn't it change the way people see God if we all found a way to get along? I think so.

Jesus only had one requirement for those who wanted to follow him. He said, "Sell all that you have, give it to the poor, and come follow me" (Matthew 19:21). He doesn't say anything about having the right beliefs, or belonging to the right group, or being ordained, or having people call you, "Reverend." He just says, sell it all and come follow me, which makes me think that none of us really gets it. I've known only one guy in my entire ministry who sold everything he had and followed Jesus. The church kicked him out.

I'll never forget it. I was a youth minister working in a big church— a huge church with stained glass windows and spires. Youth ministers never have the corner office, they're usually down in the church basement. My window was at eye level looking out on the lawn. One morning I got to work early and a guy dressed in a white robe was sleeping outside my window. He had long greasy hair, a straggly beard, and he looked like Jesus.

I waited until he woke up and asked him to come in. When he came through the door, his odor kicked me in the nostrils. I wondered if I had made a mistake. I asked him if he was homeless. He said, "Foxes have holes, birds of the air have nests, but the Son of Man has nowhere to lay his head." He was quoting Jesus (Luke 9:58).

Long story short. The guy decided to take Jesus at his word. He gave it all up, sold every possession he had. He put on a robe and decided to follow Jesus. He hit the road, living one day at a time, telling people about Jesus. I thought he was a bit of a nut, but I also thought, "I couldn't do this."

He said he was hungry. So, I gave him my sack lunch. He needed some money for a toothbrush and toothpaste. I dug in my pockets but only had a few quarters. I knew the senior pastor had arrived and was upstairs in his office. I thought for sure he would have some money to give him, so I took my new friend up to the corner office. We knocked on the door and when I opened it, the look on the pastor's face was priceless. My friend didn't look like Jesus to the pastor; he looked like a bum.

I don't know how it all started, but they got to swapping scripture passages. I was invited to leave. I felt like a Roman guard tossing my friend into the lion's den. Sitting outside, I heard a lot of arguing, mostly from the senior pastor. The janitor walked by and shook his head. He had seen it before.

I guess I wasn't too shocked when the pastor threw the Jesus man out of the church. He had done it before. The church was a hangout for a lot of folks passing through town. The pastor said he was tired of being taken advantage of by those who refused to get jobs.

Feeling like the largest hypocrite who ever followed Jesus, I slunk back to my office. Passing by the church gym, I looked over and saw the janitor and my friend in the kitchen. The janitor had cooked him some breakfast. He had pulled out his wallet and gave the Jesus man a few dollars for a toothbrush and toothpaste. They shook hands, and the Jesus man went on his way. It made me think, who was the follower of Jesus? The senior pastor or the janitor? Truly, they both are. The community that follows Jesus is comprised of both kinds of people. There are saints like the Jesus man; your average person who struggles with their shadows like the senior pastor; and the follower of Jesus who really understands—the janitor.

I'm the senior pastor now with a corner office, with the youth person in the basement. I've done enough stupid things to make that first senior pastor look like a saint. But I never forgot that the conflict was over a few dollars for toothpaste and a toothbrush. The senior pastor got to arguing theology and what he thought the scriptures meant when he should have, "kept silent and listened." It's arguments like this that drive people from following Jesus. It's sad commentary, but it's true. Many people leave churches because of similar conflicts.

Here's the thing though, if they leave what they think is "The Church" but they follow Jesus, they can't help but start talking to folks again. Before they know it, they invite each other over for dinner, they meet each other for coffee, they bring their Bibles, and they start talking and voila, "Wherever two or more are gathered there I am also" (Matthew 18:20). A dynamic energy, greater than the group, kicks in. People start telling each other about their lives. Some may ask others what they think it means to follow Jesus. Some may start crying while others listen. The conversation starts roaming to what to do about the kids hanging out at the mall. Still, others worry about war or poverty in their neighborhood. Someone asks, "What would Jesus do?" So, they dig out their Bibles and read. Suddenly they realize they have an idea or an ability that would be the perfect fit to solve this problem, so they volunteer. Before they know it, Jesus is working through them and they're points of light, acting in love, changing the way people see God. They've become the church. The Called-Out Ones. People of the Way— all born out of conflict. It is too bad people can't stay together, work through their differences, manage their shadows, act in love, and model to the world how followers of Jesus bring peace to the earth, as well as to each other.

Who's Invited to the Table?

Tom is a member of my church. He sings in our choir, and he's an elder leading the community. The spirit of God moves through Tom. He has climbed underneath people's crosses and carried them when things got rough. He is a light shining in the darkness, he serves in love, he changes the way people see God. He's gay.

Tom became a member of our community when he was thrown out of another one because he's gay. In his other community people loved him and enjoyed his singing. Tom became comfortable with them and eventually came out to them. They were shocked.

His community couldn't understand how someone like Tom could be gay. They encouraged him to go into therapy, to change, to become what God intended him to be—straight. When Tom tried to share that this was how God made him, they disagreed. They pointed to the Bible passages where they believed it said that being gay was an abomination. He was asked to leave the community. Tom was heart-broken. He had joined a community, claiming to follow Jesus, and when he shared who he was, they booted him out.

It was all about scripture, or so they said. Yes, there are seven places in the Bible that speak about different forms of homosexuality—or so people think. As I shared in the Path of the Bible, these passages are interpreted incorrectly. These seven passages are historically locked, and they don't apply to us today. By booting LGBTQ people out of communities of faith we're missing not only the gifts they offer, but we're not following one of the teachings of Jesus.

Jesus taught a parable about a wealthy man who gave a great banquet. He spent a large sum of money to make sure the table was loaded with food and all the decorations were beautiful. When all the preparations were finished, the wealthy man sent his servants to invite the guests to his feast. One by one the guests turned down the wealthy man with a series of excuses. When the wealthy man heard this, he sent his servants out to all the highways and side streets. He said, "Go out quickly into the streets and alleys of the town and bring the poor, the crippled, the blind, and the lame." Or in our terms, "bring in the gay, straight, and anybody else we would cast aside." The servant went and did as the master said. But he reported to the wealthy man, "There's still room!" The master then told his servant, "Go out to the roads and country lanes and compel them to come in, so that my house will be full!" Or in our context, we might say, "Bring in the Jew, the Muslim, and the Buddhist!" (Luke 14:25-24).

I like to imagine that the master's banquet hall was packed with all different types of people, many of whom we may say aren't following Jesus. But the master didn't care about the labels we put on people. Notice that none of those who attended the feast had to profess a belief in Jesus, they didn't have to sign a confession of faith or adhere to doctrines. They were invited, they came, and they enjoyed the master's feast.

Jesus's parable teaches what the communities who follow him are to be like. Those who follow Jesus are to create communities where all are invited to come; peasant, the middle class, and the wealthy class. Everyone, regardless of wealth or privilege, is part of the body of Christ and all parts of the body are equal. Their love "does not insist on its own way." These communities of faith don't pay attention to sexual differences, gender, nationalities, or religious affiliations. All of them are invited to use their gifts. If women have the gift of preaching, teaching, and leading, then they are assigned those tasks. If men have the gift of care, service, and working with children, then they are given those tasks. When communities of faith act in this way, they change the way people see God. They model that God embraces the entire world. This is what communities of Jesus create when they come together. It's Paul's vision for the church and was grounded in what he believed Jesus taught. It's the pattern we should follow.

Unfortunately, there are many followers of Jesus who object to this open acceptance of all and have stopped reading this book; I crossed a line, I went too far. I guess that's why there are so many denominations. Also, if they're not careful, they may become like my senior pastor, and boot the Jesus man right out the door of the church when he should be given the seat of honor.

As you contemplate joining a community, I encourage you to find one that is inclusive of all people. It should be led by people with gifts, regardless of orientations or genders. Everybody should be welcome.

Join Something

To practice this Jesus Path, you're going to want to be a part of something. It could be a Bible group, a prayer group, a group that meditates, or a group that marches for social causes in Jesus's name. You might join a church on a corner or one with a steeple. Or perhaps one that meets in a school, a mall, a living room, a megadome, a bar, or a coffee shop. You might want to join a church on Facebook and follow each other on Instagram or Snapchat. A community following Jesus on Social Media is as profound as a church meeting in person. Often a virtual church is more inclusive as it transcends national and cultural borders.

Whatever community you join, remember, none is perfect. Leave your stones at the door. Be humble and pray for wisdom. Keep silent and listen. Jesus needs us to be together. We make Jesus alive for each other when we carry each other's crosses, dry each other's tears, and invite all to the table—we change the way people see God.

Chapter Seven: The Path of Compassion

I know an angel. You would never know it by looking at him. He doesn't have a halo. He doesn't glow. He's skinny as a stick with a pale aura about him. He doesn't wear flowing robes; rather he wears his uniform of blue pants and a white shirt with his name stitched on a name patch. His vinyl pocket protector is weighted down with pens, pencils, and a small screwdriver. He's not a pastor, professor, or an orator, yet he has healing powers. He can mend anything mechanical.

My fridge was deader than a doornail. He came, laid on hands, and I prayed the bill wouldn't be too high. He took it apart, fixed the motor, and like Lazarus rising from the tomb, my fridge came back from the dead. It was nothing short of a miracle.

The sign stenciled on the side of his truck says it all, "Repairman." I've told him his true identity is a "Repairer of Men."

Every Thursday night my friend, the "repairer of men," works at a coffee shop for inner-city campers. These folks who camp under bridges, along hedges, and in large culverts, make their way to the coffee shop where my friend makes them peanut butter and jelly sandwiches. The campers come in droves, pushing their carts loaded with all their earthly belongings. My friend gives them a sandwich, a cup of coffee, and a smile. While the rest of us step over and around them, when they come to the coffee shop, my friend calls each of them by name.

It is not a clean or easy job. The campers make quite a mess. The smoke hangs thick in the room like a bad day in L.A. Their rumpled coats have the sour tinge of old booze. More than once my friend broke up quarrels. Once he had to call the police when one of the campers passed out, drunk on the spot. But he is with them Thursday in and Thursday out.

Slowly, slowly over the years, the campers came to trust him. They tell him their stories. He listens, smiles, and hands them a sandwich. He doesn't try to convert, proselytize, or evangelize. No one must hear a sermon before they get their sandwich and coffee. What happens in that coffee shop is nothing short of miraculous. Stitch by stitch, sandwich by sandwich; you can hear as the camper's souls are sewn together.

Salvation is the furthest thing from my friend's mind. He doesn't care for the campers to get into heaven. He just says he's following Jesus. The compassion my friend shows by taking care of the inner-city camper is exactly what Jesus would say we must do to be his faithful follower.

The Divine Open Sesame

I believe in universal salvation. God has saved every human who ever walked, or will walk, the planet. I can't imagine a good, loving, and gracious God would ever reject someone she created. It's hard to point to a specific passage in the Bible or a doctrine in the church to prove my point; I just know God saved all of us. Through Jesus, God was doing something unique and miraculous by reconciling the entire world so all would be part of God's kingdom. But other followers of Jesus disagree with me.

Some followers of Jesus are obsessed with trying to figure out who's saved and who's not. As I've shared in several other paths, they argue incessantly over the rules and qualifications of salvation. Some say salvation is only for those who profess, "I believe in Jesus as my Lord and Savior." With these words, they think the gates of heaven open like Ali Baba chanting, "Open Sesame." Some followers of Jesus want a statement of faith, long lists of doctrines, or hoops of theology to jump through before someone is saved, secured, and locked into going to heaven. Other followers of Jesus say you were never saved in the first place if you argue, question, doubt, or engage in destructive behavior.

In Matthew's Gospel, Jesus teaches about salvation. In these passages, we need to take Jesus seriously, not literally. Jesus was trying to make a point about compassion. In this Gospel Jesus said it will be a great surprise who is saved and who isn't. He said many won't make it into heaven on judgment day and will be shocked because they knew their place in heaven was all sewn up. When facing their judgment, they will say to Jesus, "Lord, Lord, did we not prophesy in your name, cast out demons in your name, and do many deeds of power in your name?" Jesus responded by saying to them, "I never knew you, go away from me, you evil doers" (Matthew 7:21). Doing things, and saying things, all in the name of Jesus is no guarantee you're saved.

Jesus said there's only one thing guaranteeing salvation "Only the one who does the will of my Father in heaven" (Matthew 17:23). So, if casting out demons in Jesus name isn't the will of God, or if doing deeds of power in Jesus name isn't the Will of God, then what is? Jesus taught another parable to answer this question. It's called the Great Judgment (Matthew 25:31).

On the final judgment day, Jesus comes and separates all of humanity into sheep and goats. I love to imagine this scene—all the people of creation turned into bleating chaos. Jesus then turns to the sheep and tells them to enter the Kingdom of God, prepared for them before the world began. The sheep are shocked, even bewildered—they are sheep and get to go to heaven? They asked Jesus why they are saved. He replied that they have this eternal reward because they fed and clothed him, gave him something to drink, visited him in prison, and took care of him. In their shock the sheep ask, "When did we see you so needy and took care of you?" Jesus said, "Whenever you did it to the least of these, my brothers and sisters you did it to me."

By the same notion, Jesus turns to the goats telling them they are cursed and are to depart into eternal fire prepared for the devil and his angels. Jesus tells the goats they never fed and clothed him, gave him something to drink, visited him when he was sick or in prison, or took care of him. The goats, genuinely surprised said, "When did we not do these things for you Lord?" Jesus says, "Whenever you didn't do it for the least of my brothers and sisters you didn't do it for me. Get away from me you evil doers."

Many interpret this parable as Jesus saying there is a hell with a devil and people will go there. I disagree. As I share in the Path of Managing the Shadow, I don't believe in a devil or hell. I also don't believe God is going to judge people, separate them, and cast them away. I can't emphasize the point enough; we must take this parable seriously, not literally. We must interpret it.

The message of this parable is compassion. The difference between the sheep and goats is that one cared and the other didn't. The sheep showed compassion to the least, the lowest of Jesus's brothers and sisters, and the goats didn't.

If followers of Jesus are going to argue about salvation, they need to know it has nothing to do with knowing Jesus's name, or doing powerful things in his name. Jesus just wants to know if they've shown compassion for the least of his brothers and sisters.

There are some followers of Jesus who adamantly disagree with this concept. They say salvation has everything to do with believing in

Jesus's name. They dedicate their entire faith to getting people to accept Jesus, to pray in his name, and to do things in Jesus name. I believe considering these teachings of Jesus . . .

They're just plain wrong.

Don't let them tell you otherwise. Point to this page in the book, or to Jesus's parable in the Bible. People can twist the story any way they want, but it still comes down to what the sheep gave and what the goats didn't give—compassion. So, while I don't believe you can earn your way into heaven, or some are saved, and some are not, you need to pay attention to the central core of Jesus's teaching—compassion. If you're going to follow Jesus, you need to show compassion.

We show compassion to all of Jesus's people, especially strangers, when we feed and clothe them, quench their thirst, visit them when they are sick, and when in prison. The cry of the goats is, "Lord if we had seen *you,* of course we would have taken you to McDonalds. But we never saw you, all we saw were street campers." The words are not even out of the goat's mouth before Jesus condemns them.

Of course we would feed Jesus. It is easy to show compassion to Jesus. He's divine, holy, and he's clean. The challenge is to show compassion to the lowest, the most abused humans on the planet, the least of Jesus's brothers and sisters. They are the ones crippled by circumstances in both body and soul.

So, who are the least of Jesus's brothers and sisters? I don't know about you, but I suddenly have a huge desire to make peanut butter and jelly sandwiches. Are the least of Jesus's brothers and sister homeless inner-city campers? Yes, they are. Are they poor folks who live in the parts of the city we'd rather not live? Yes, they could be also. Do they live in a distant third world country and are victims of oppression and injustice, or refugees from war? They would be considered as well. Are they Wall Street brokers in high-end silk business suits driving a Lexus? Believe it or not, they could also be considered the least of Jesus's brothers and sisters for we don't know the pain and broken hearts they might be carrying. The least would be anyone you may meet. Anybody, at any time, is the least of Jesus's brothers and sisters. This is why followers of Jesus show compassion to everyone.

True North

I love the word "Compassion." The root is compass. To know the way to follow Jesus, we hold a spiritual compass in front of us. If we get lost or confused about what it means to follow Jesus, our compass shows us true north. The compass shows compassion, always pointing to Jesus. If we want to know what it means to follow Jesus, we will find the least of Jesus's brothers and sisters; we hold up the compass of our faith and show them compassion.

We don't know the contents of other people's souls, and we don't know the burdens other people bare, so potentially everyone reflects the least of these. That's why the place to start showing compassion is the face you see in the mirror.

Spiritual Back Yards

People remind me of homes in a new subdivision. As you drive down Main Street, each house has a gorgeous front yard. The front lawn is manicured with the same two bushes and the same spindly tree. The street side of each home has the appearance of a well put together home. The true story lies behind the cedar picket fence. The backyards are a mess. They're muddy and filled with construction equipment. The real work to be done is in the back. It's the same with people.

We put on a façade saying to our neighbors and the world that everything is great, we're fine, and our lives are secure. But when we step into the backyard of our lives, things are a mess. Some of us have marriages that are a shamble of weeds. Others have kids that are a tangled swing set of emotions. Many have jobs that are a pile of bricks they've carried for years.

Each of us has pain and brokenness; a significant burden weighing us down. So, the first person to show compassion to is ourselves. I've seen many followers of Jesus who bestow tremendous compassion on others but harbor deep pain and guilt in their own lives. They miss the part in the great commandment where Jesus says to love God and our neighbors as we love ourselves. We're God's children and God desires that we love ourselves. We are good, whole, wonderful, and beautiful. To follow Jesus, we need to accept God's grace in our lives and receive forgiveness in our souls.

Forgiveness is one of the most profound parts of what it means to follow Jesus. As we are forgiven, so we bestow forgiveness on others. Jesus taught his disciples to constantly forgive. One of the disciples asked Jesus if he should forgive his brother as much as seven times. Jesus said he was to forgive him as much as seventy times seven, which was a colloquial way of saying, "constantly." Jesus knew we'd be stepping on each other's toes and hearts. To stay sane, whole, and balanced, Jesus, in his wisdom, taught that we must be people of forgiveness.

Stupid Cows

Many people misunderstand the meaning of forgiveness. Lewis Smedes in his book, *The Art of Forgiveness,* (Ballentine. 1996) teaches the basics of this divine skill. Smeads describes that forgiveness is not an impulsive action. We don't shake hands and forgive. We don't kiss and make up. We don't forgive and let evil people back into our lives. We can forgive people and still hold them accountable. Forgiveness is a long, slow process involving remembering, dialogue, holding people accountable, and eventually letting go and finding peace.

Forgiveness is not something we only grant to someone else, but it's something we give to ourselves. When we're able to forgive we let go of the bile, the hatred, and the anger in our lives because of the violence that's been done to us. Forgiveness is central to healing, especially when we're the ones who inflict violence on ourselves.

We've all committed a pile of mistakes. Our spiritual backyard is a grave filled with bones from the road kill of our lives. We bury one skeleton after another. We continue layering dirt over the bones hoping that if we cover our pain deep enough, it will go away. It doesn't. Our souls are like the soil that forces rocks to the surface. The bones of our past mistakes keep surfacing until we deal with them.

I know of only one way to deal with the bones—forgiveness. We must engage in the process of forgiveness in our lives. We have to look in the mirror, think of Jesus loving us as we are and accept it. Forgiveness begins with us.

Forgiveness is like drinking a cool glass of water. It's like wearing a warm coat, or enjoying a meal, or getting out of prison. It's a peanut butter and jelly sandwich for your soul. When we're able to accept God's forgiveness, we are overcome with a deep and profound sense of joy.

When we realize God accepts and forgives us, we can strive to be better people. It is what unconditional love does to us. Some think unconditional love allows us to settle into a complacent acceptance of our negative attitudes and behavior; the opposite is true. When we feel complete, unconditional love—God's love—we are motivated to achieve our potential.

Look in the mirror. Look at your face, the lines and crinkles around your eyes. Gaze into your eyes and see your entire life history. This is how God views you. God loves you just as you are. God has compassion for you. Accept it.

OK I get it. You can't do this. You're not the first one who is unable to forgive themselves. So, pick up your sorry self and go to your closet. Find all the clothes you haven't worn in a year. Face it, you're never going to wear them again. Put them all in a garbage bag. Now go to your pantry and grab some of those plastic grocery bags you've chosen over paper. Bag half your canned corn, hash, pinto beans, and boxed macaroni.

Now haul your stuff to the Salvation Army. Put the stuff on the counter. Don't ask for a tax receipt. You're not doing this for your taxes; you're doing this for your heart. This is one way to knead your old heart like someone making dough. Now watch what happens. You'll smile.

Now really suck it up. Volunteer at the Salvation Army. Take one evening a month and serve soup at an inner-city mission. Volunteer to read books at the corner preschool. Find some way to lose yourself.

It's an oxymoron. I love that word. It sounds like a stupid cow; oxy-moron. Now some think this is exactly what you are if you follow Jesus and start losing yourself. You'll do things that just don't make sense. You'll be a living oxymoron. Jesus said to find yourself you must lose yourself, to save a life, you must lose your life (Matthew 16:25). Following Jesus is a contradiction in terms, but it's the only way to find joy.

If you can't look in the mirror and forgive yourself; then you need to go out and be with others. Get involved—totally involved. Become so involved your schedule is packed full and you'll wonder if you'll ever have time for yourself. That's the whole idea. Lose yourself.

When you're busy reading to kids, listening to seniors, dishing out food at the homeless shelter, serving on the board at the local "Y," going to some distant country to build homes, sitting and listening quietly to someone who's hurting, something happens. Your heart begins to soften. When you become lost in the pain and sorrow of someone's life, it touches the pain in your own. When you sit with someone who has shed tears, tell them how important, loved, and valuable they are to God. When they smile and tell you that you've given them hope for another day, something happens to you.

Once again, you'll end up in the bathroom looking in the mirror with your arms on the sink edge supporting yourself like two jacks lifting an old truck. You'll look in the mirror and ask, "If I can say it to others, why can't I say it to myself? I'm important and loved. God values me." Jesus is right. If you lose yourself, you'll find yourself. You'll be the stupid cow, the oxymoron. You will find compassion for your own soul.

Gnarled Toes

Jesus constantly struggled to show the disciples what it meant to love each other and follow him. So, one night after their dinner together, Jesus got up, took off his outer garments, wrapped a towel around his waist, and with a basin of water, washed the feet of each disciple. When he finished, he said to them, "If I your lord and teacher have washed your feet, you also ought to wash each other's feet. For I have set you an example that you should do as I have done to you" (John 13:12). It is the greatest and highest calling we have as followers of Jesus. We are to live in such a way that we wash each other's feet.

There is a shower at the coffee house where my friend works. They supply the soap, shampoo, and towels. The campers line up to get their weekly bath. I like to imagine Jesus is with them checking to make sure they have washed behind their ears and between their toes.

Jesus couldn't make it any clearer. "A new commandment that I give you, that you love one another. Just as I have loved you, so should you love one another. By this everyone will know that you are my disciples if you have love for one another" (John 13:34,35). This new commandment supersedes all that has come before it. It is greater than the law and the prophets of the Hebrew Bible. It is the highest teaching of the New Testament. It all comes down to this.

Love

If we want to follow Jesus, we will love one another as he loved us. What does this love look like? Jesus said, "No one has greater love than this, to lay down one's life for one's friends. You are my friends if you do what I command you" (John 15:13; 14). There it is again, a command. Jesus commands us to love another to the point of sacrificing our lives. This is why salvation is so much more than "believing in Jesus." Salvation is for those who go beyond mere belief and put their lives where their hearts are. Compassion is the greatest challenge and the highest calling. Therefore, you must go beyond showing compassion for yourself and get involved in the world.

Think right now, who would you say is the least of Jesus's brothers and sisters? Quick, don't filter it, just let it come. Who is it? Your ex, your children, the in-laws, kids down the street, old folks in nursing homes, inner-city campers, or people living in the slums of El Salvador? Remember it could be anyone. I guarantee whoever comes to your mind are the ones Jesus is asking you to show compassion for.

These are the people whose feet you must wash. They could be the ones you must forgive.

It costs you, no doubt about it. It costs you time, money, and energy. It costs you emotion and pain. Loving the least of Jesus's brothers and sisters is difficult work. When you wash people's feet you'll wonder how they got their calluses and scars. You'll see how their toes are broken and ask why their shoes are torn. You'll start asking questions about how they got to this point in their life. It doesn't take long before the love you feel for Jesus is transferred into indignation for how other children of God could be treated so poorly. The love you have for Jesus, his command to love one another, will be more than making peanut butter and jelly sandwiches. It may also include working to find ways of ending gang violence that threatens the street campers; work for legislation to build shelters for them; find them employment to hopefully get them off the street and into permanent safe housing. When you wash other people's feet you are motivated to petition city hall, walk on Washington, or fly to distant countries. You'll be changed.

Compassion does not make you popular. People will think you're crazy for wasting your time. You'll be the stupid cow, the oxymoron. They may even begin to curse you. It's called the cost of discipleship. High-rent apartments now surround the coffee shop where my friend serves the campers. The new neighbors don't like the campers and their carts full of their belongings—the rent values are lowered. They'd like the coffee shop to move. The coffee shop owners love Jesus. For them it's not just a job, it's not just coffee, it's doing what Jesus commanded them to do. They feel called by Jesus to stay where they are.

Jesus anticipated that showing compassion brings pain. This is why he said, "Blessed are you when people revile you and persecute you and utter all kinds of evil against you falsely on my account. Rejoice and be glad, for your reward will be great in heaven" (Matthew 5:11-13). Compassion is not always easy. But if you're tarred and feathered and run out of town, I guarantee there will be a smile on your face. You smile, you feel joy because for the first time in your life you have found yourself. You found the great divine self you were meant to be. The feeling will be angelic.

What would you do if an angel from God suddenly appeared to you? Wouldn't you roll out the spiritual red carpet and fall all over yourself, bowing and curtsying? Don't you think you'd go rigid with respect? Of course, you would. They're angels. They're holy. God expects nothing less. You need to think about these angels from God the next time you want to curse the face in the mirror, the face on the street, or the face on the other side of the world. The author of the book of Hebrews teaches that we should never tire of showing compassion to the strangers around us, for we never know when we are attending to angels unaware (Hebrews 13:2).

I love that image, angels unaware. I can just see the angels who visit my friends at the coffee house. Before they turn the corner on the block, they quickly tuck their wings into their ratty coat. They muss up each other's hair, throw dirt on their faces, and wrinkle their robes. They light up cigarettes and stumble through the door.

My friend greets them by name. He takes their coats and gives them a cup of coffee and a peanut butter and jelly sandwich. My friend doesn't see homeless vagrants, but men and women, children of God. He cares for them because he knows who they really are, angels.

Chapter Eight: The Path of Prayer

I have an ache for God. I can't describe it any other way. I ache, my heart hurts. I feel like a homesick twelve-year-old stuck at camp. I want to call, to connect with my parents, to sleep in my bed. This ache draws me into prayer and silence. It settles into my soul, and I stare out my window like a child inside on a rainy day. I take out my journal and write to my father who has passed away.

Sometimes I miss my Dad so much that I ache. We lived in different states. I lived in Colorado, and he lived in Oregon. We saw each other a couple times a year. I remember the last time I saw him— we hugged each other, never knowing when we would see each other again. So, this hug would have to last. I still feel the imprint of my father's arms on my shoulders, which keeps me going when I'm lonely for my Dad.

It is the same with God. Before we were born, God hugged our souls because he knew it would be a while before we would be in complete union. This hug is a divine imprint on the depths of our being. God gripped us in a deep, long embrace leaving his holy impression on us. God then bids us goodbye and slips us into the world.

The mark God left on me is part of my creation as a human. I can feel it like I feel my father's last hug. When I'm lost and unsure of where I'm going, this divine imprint reminds me of my true identity as a child of God—I belong to God.

The divine imprint causes this ache. While it draws me closer to God, it also reminds me of the distance between us. The ache is never satisfied until God and I are one and embrace after death in resurrection. Until then, I am mindful of God's impression on my life.

Joy does this for me. Talking with my wife, racing down a hillside on a mountain bike, flashing a fly line across a slip of river, losing myself in a chorus of people singing, or ministering to those who hurt; these things give me joy touching the divine imprint. Even in the joy, the ache deepens as I draw closer to God. The pain only eases when I sit in silence, close my eyes, and pray with the one who left this divine impression on my soul, my Holy Poppa.

The Holy Poppa

As a toddler, I had a blanket with edges rimmed with silk. I remember waking up and climbing out of my crib. Dragging my blanket behind me, I'd toddle down the hallway in my footie pajamas, lie down over the heater vent, and pull my blanket over me, the silk against my cheek. When the heater kicked on I'd fall asleep in a cozy tent of PJs, blanket, and silk. The next thing I knew, I was scooped up in my father's huge arms who wrapped the blanket around me.

Each day my father carried me through his morning routine. I remember the smell of Folgers instant coffee, the buzz of an electric razor, and blue Aqua Velva.

I have a similar routine as an adult. While still dark I awaken and wrap myself in an orange quilt my grandmother knitted me before she died. My PJs don't have plastic feet anymore, but they're blue sweats, ratty from years of washing. Sipping coffee, I sit warm beside the wood stove. Bowing in prayer, I feel the ache even this early in the morning. I close my eyes and wait in silence. God comes and carries me as my father did.

It happens quite often. As I'm praying, in my mind's eye I'm three, and have been scooped up in divine arms and placed on God's broad shoulders. I can feel God's hair. I grip God's chin for balance.

It happened this morning. It's been a long few days, leaving me confused and frustrated. I woke up in the middle of the night, grabbed my quilt and came out to the couch. I began praying, the wood stove warm with glowing embers. What I saw in my head was like watching a movie, but I was in the movie. God came out of the darkness and suddenly, God and I are walking down a trail through tall weeds. I don't know this trail, but I know God knows the way. My eyes open and the message is clear. I'm ok. I feel peace. I'm not in control, God is, and I must hang on for the ride. I crawl back into bed and fall asleep. When I wake up there is a deep peace that comes from being with my heavenly Dad. The ache is eased, and I'm able to live the day.

The Homesick Jesus

Jesus had a deep ache for God. God put a divine imprint on Jesus's life leaving him homesick. You see it in how he prays. The Bible translates the word Jesus uses when he addresses God as "Father." The translators have it wrong; it's way too formal. The appropriate translation in the Aramaic, (the language spoken by Jesus) is more personal and intimate, "Dad, Pop, Poppa." When Jesus felt his ache, he withdrew from the others to pray to his Dad. In the Garden of Gethsemane, before Jesus is arrested, we see the intensity of this relationship. When I read this passage, it is like listening in on a one-sided conversation between father and son as they discuss a painful issue. "Dad, if it's possible, please let this pass from me. Yet, Dad, please, I want to do what you want me to do." "Dad, if this cannot pass unless I do this, then I want you to know, I will do what you want" (Matthew 26:39, 42, paraphrase).

My heart breaks as I read this passage. I know that it is just as painful for the silent voice on the other end. It reminds me of a young man in the military making one last call home before entering the war zone. He aches to connect with his parents, knowing it may be the last time. He is a son who wants his parents to know he's afraid, yet he knows what he must do.

What does a father say in such a conversation? Does he tell his son to be brave? Does he tell his son not to be frightened? Does he tell his son that he loves him? I hope so. I hope this is what God told Jesus in Gethsemane. I hope God told Jesus he was loved, he wasn't alone, and that he was with him. I wanted Jesus to know before he died that his Poppa loved him and had not abandoned him.

I think God ached for Jesus in Gethsemane. I know God didn't set up Jesus to die this way. God intended Jesus to be the Savior, but not like this, not in such a brutal way, not through crucifixion. But Jesus confronted an intense evil that wanted to destroy him. Evil wanted Jesus dead, and would not settle for anything less than a dead body in a sealed tomb. I believe it pained God that he could not stop the evil surrounding Jesus. Like a father who could not stop a son from going into battle, God could not stop Jesus from facing his death.

What happened to Jesus also happens to us. It's how God, in great wisdom, set up the world. We have free will. Our choices have consequences, implications, and ramifications. At other times, choices are made for us. Evil people break into our lives, accidents happen, or natural events occur, putting our lives out of control. Our lives are a confusing mess of choices and consequences.

As each new event breaks into our lives, we must discern what God wants us to do. We must choose the path where God wants us to go. We must live with courage and faithfulness, and boldly choose what we feel will bring God's kingdom to earth. We must choose for compassion, justice, forgiveness, and joy. It's hard, but we need to get past the evil done to us. The choices we face are often difficult, painful, and confusing. Our choices are rarely black and white; instead, our choices are shades of gray. We ache for direction amid these choices and yearn for God to somehow intervene in our lives. This ache for God drives us to prayer. Prayer touches the depths of our being and touches God's impression on us. We move into God's presence through prayer.

God sees our battles and pain. God desires to guide, encourage, and comfort us. He sways us to choose God's Will. God aches when our choices deviate from God's intentions. It hurts God when we are victims of circumstances or the evil choices of others. This ache drives God to be present to us through every means possible.

God aches. We ache. It's why we pray, fast, journal, and spend time in quiet. We do these things to be with God, so our hearts become one with God's heart.

Unplug

I have visions where God reveals my purpose in life, directions I'm supposed to take, and things God wants me to say. God shows me exactly what to do. In the Path of Resurrection, I share my vision of heaven. I know what happens to us after we die. I've seen visions of heaven; lush meadows, dense green forests filled with birds and animals, and throngs of people enjoying God's presence. It's paradise. God speaks to me as plainly as a person would. God also speaks to me in the center of my head. It is not my conscious speaking to me; my conscious voice is distinctly different. God's voice is outside of me speaking to the inside of me. When I hear God speak, there is a profound sense of a divine presence.

God's voice is soothing, calm, and full of encouragement. It is like my father's voice talking to me before my little league basketball game. I was so nervous I'd want to vomit. My dad reminded me that I knew what I was doing, to stay calm, and to trust my instincts. He reminded me that God was with me, and I wasn't alone. It was just a basketball game. But when you're a tall, skinny, pimply-faced eighth-grader, making the basketball team was the only thing that mattered.

I'll never forget one incident. My dad picked me up after practice and I cried as I told him I wanted to be dead, I was so disappointed. He pulled the Buick over to talk to me. "Your life is more than basketball or making the team. You are valuable to your mother and me. We love you whether or not you're on the team. You're God's child and our child." It eased my feeling of failure, and I finally stopped crying.

As life evolved into young adulthood, I was dealing with all the complexities of choosing my way. I had to face my own Gethsemanes. In these times, I was driven to prayer. While the times of absolute silence left me terrified, I also heard God's soothing voice encourage and remind me that my life was valuable. I am loved. God told me my life was more than an existential line of one day after another. The pain eased, and I found the courage to reach out and live another day.

Now maybe I've just incorporated my Dad's voice into my head and projected it onto God. If so, it shows the powerful influence a positive parent has in the life of a child. A therapist may say I'm hearing my Super Ego adopt my father's voice as an interior dialogue with my Ego. After I've shared my visions, people sometimes tell me I'm delusional. They look at me like I've lost my mind, or that I'm three bricks shy of a load, or I'm not all there. But I don't think so. I bet my life on my visions. While the voice is like my Dad's, it's not his voice, it's a divine other. I hear God's voice in my head and feel the divine trying to sooth my ache.

People are curious why God speaks to me and not to them. Some speculate that I hear God because I'm a minister. Believe me, that is not the case. You don't have to be a saint to hear God's voice, you just have to want to.

I hear God's voice because I want, desire, and long to. I want it so badly that I eliminate things from my life to make room, I clear the clutter, noise, people; anything muffling God's voice. Think about your morning routine. If you're typical, you flip something on, a radio, television, or computer. Right out of the chute we listen to the radio DJ cracking stupid jokes to wake us up. Others check emails or grab the newspaper and spend time reading the paper.

Then we get in our cars and do what? We flip on the radio to listen to a DJ or more news. We turn on our phones and fill our cars with sound. We get to work, and we are surrounded by phones, schedules, computers, talking, chattering- a constant cacophony of noise.

After work, we jump back into our cars and flip the radio on again to listen to the DJ or more news. Or we listen to our phones and more music, anything to fill the forty-five-minute, mind-numbing commute in rush-hour traffic.

At home, the first thing we do is turn something else back on. The TV, (as if something's changed in the last ten minutes) or our computer to check email. We flip through the snail mail, start dinner, pop open a beer, or uncork a bottle of wine. Many of us eat dinner listening to the news.

After dinner, we watch more TV—sitcoms or news shows. We surf the net, write emails, watch kitten videos, or swap internet jokes. We then fight to stay awake until the evening news hoping to make it to the weather report or maybe sports. We have timers on our TV, so it turns off after we've fallen asleep.

We sleep, the alarm goes off, once again the annoying DJ wakes us up, and we start the entire process again.

Studies show that the average North American spends at least eight hours a day interacting with some form of media. Let's face it; we're addicted. We're junkies. We're hooked on gossip masquerading as important information. We need the noise in our lives because we're lonely. We seek the sound of other voices to keep us from facing ourselves.

God doesn't compete with the noise. I hate this about God and wish he were more aggressive, willing to grab us by our spiritual collars, look us in the eyes, and shout above the din, "Look here, look at me, listen to me!" But God doesn't. God is silent. God is more than willing to take a back seat in your life. God stays in the background, quiet, hidden, and waiting for a relationship.

God would love to have a conversation. God would love to talk—aches to talk. But unfortunately, we're plugged into so much noise we can't hear God. So, God will wait . . . for years, even a lifetime.

Sometimes people are lucky. When they see a glorious sunrise tinged with gold and orange as they commute, they're so mesmerized they turn off the DJ to just wonder in the moment. God grabs moments like this to sneak in a casual, albeit not so humble observation, "See, don't I do good work?" If they're lucky, they'll stop for a moment and begin thinking about God, about life, and about who they are amid this immense and glorious sunrise.

Others are not so lucky. A major crisis comes careening into their lives; a car wreck, a heart attack, a pink slip at work, or the death of a child, parent, or friend. Their lives swerve into an existential fence post forcing them to scream, "Where is God? How could God let this happen to me?"

God uses moments like these as well. During the pain, anguish, despair, and death, God speaks two quiet words, "I'm here." The choice is ours. We can wait for the sunrise, we can wait for the cataclysmic collision, or we can choose right now to make room in our lives to hear God. We can turn something off, tune something out, and unplug from the technology bombarding us. We can alter our lives by breaking the news addiction and carving out time to do things that attune our ears to God. I call it moving into the divine strike zone.

Fore!

I live in the Rocky Mountains and we're bombarded with powerful thunder and lightning storms every summer. If you want to witness the power of the universe, come to Colorado. The thunderheads boil and build at three o'clock in the afternoon like clock-work. When the storm strikes, you know you're just bug spit on the windshield of life.

What would I do if I wanted to be hit by lightning? What are my chances of being struck if I took a golf club, went to my basement, stood in the bathtub, wore rubber boots and heavy lineman gloves, held the club over my head, and yelled, "Go ahead God, strike me dead?" If God was in the right mood she might just fire a bolt at my house, but chances are I'd be safe.

Now, what happens if I took that same golf club and played a round at three o'clock in the afternoon? If I lift my club to the heavens while the thunderheads boom and everyone else runs for the clubhouse and yell, "Go ahead God, strike me dead! I dare you! Fore!" I just painted a divine bull's eye on my head that is just too good for God to pass up.

I call it, "The Divine Strike Zone." Not that hearing God is like being hit by lighting, although sometimes it can be. God has zapped me with his insights many times. But if we want to hear God, we need to enhance our ability to hear God. We need to move into the divine strike zone—unplug from the noise, quiet ourselves, and do what Jesus did, pray.

Go into Your Closet

Before I wrote these words, I spent time in prayer. First, I went to the place in my home called, "my sacred place." In the winter, it's beside the wood stove. In the summer I sit in the sunroom filled with plants bathed in sunshine. Sometimes I sit outside in my bird sanctuary where I have numerous feeders for the Jays, Chickadees, and Nuthatches that come while I pray. Today I was in the sunroom. My dog is curled up in the sun rays across the floor. Turning my chair toward the window, I repeat a mantra I've used for years, "Lord Jesus Christ, son of God, have mercy on me." This mantra, called the Jesus prayer, was used back in the fourth century. I quiet myself, the mantra spinning through my head, as it begins to quiet, my mind. I feel a gentle peace opening to the spirit of God.

After several moments of quiet, I take the Bible and read a passage from a devotional guide I've used for years. I begin *Lectio Divina* described in the Path on the Bible.

I read the passage, kiss the pages, and I return to my Mantra.

I read the passage again and allow it to read me. I allow the words of God to resonate in my soul. I kiss the pages, set the Bible back down in my lap, and repeat the Mantra.

I take the Bible a third time, reading the same passage. I listen and wait for God. I kiss the passage and set the Bible back down in my lap and return to my Mantra.

Reading the Bible in a *Lectio* style is so powerful that if you do nothing else in this Jesus Path, I recommend it. God speaks through the scriptures to you.

After several moments of quiet, I feel peace in my body. The repetition of the Mantra stops. I roll through the process of prayer. I pour out to God the aches of my heart. I begin thanking God for the wonderful aspects of life and living in this amazing world. After giving thanks, my prayers roll to supplication. I list the things I need from God.

From supplication, I begin prayers of intercession. I list those I want God to bless. I pray for God's blessing on my family. I pray early before my family wakes. I imagine Jesus going to my bedroom where my wife sleeps. I imagine Jesus sitting down on the edge of our bed and laying his hands upon my wife. I pray that Jesus will bless her and bless our marriage. I imagine Jesus going to my children's homes. I picture Jesus sitting on the edge of their beds, laying hands on their heads. I ask Jesus to guard and guide them. One is a firefighter, one a physical therapist, and the other a park ranger. I ask Jesus to protect them. I pray that Jesus fills me with the wisdom to be a good and faithful father.

My prayers turn towards my mother and mother-in-law. I ask for God's blessing on their lives. I pray for each of my siblings, their spouses, and my nieces and nephews. My daily morning prayers connect our family who are scattered across the western United States. Praying for my family takes fifteen minutes. To practice this Jesus Path, I encourage you to take a sacred fifteen minutes and pray for your family and friends.

I move to prayers of intercession for the planet. I imagine the world as a shining globe in my hands. Spinning the globe, I feel it turn slowly in my imagination. I pray for nations, world leaders, and individuals suffering from wars, famine, and oppression.

Slowly, the desire for intervention subsides, and my prayers turn towards praise. I praise God for the glory of the cosmos, the far-flung galaxies, black holes, and the absolute mystery of creation.

Next, I spend time just listening for God. It's quiet; I've moved into "the strike zone." I simply listen for God. Sometimes God speaks. Other times it's quiet. If nothing else, quiet is good.

I close my prayers by bowing before God—bending my head towards the ground. I submit to God. I dedicate this new day to God. I commit myself to God's Will. I promise to minister to everyone who comes my way, either through the intention of my schedule or the happenstance of life.

Time is always a crunch for me. There are days when I could pray this way for hours. However, I usually only have one hour to give. I feel jealous of the great mystics who prayed for two to three hours a day. I long for this and hope it will be possible someday. But it won't be this day. I need to cook breakfast and get out the door. An early morning appointment waits for me at the office and thus the day begins.

Jesus expected his followers to be people of prayer. When he taught his disciples how to pray he said, "When you pray. . . ," notice it wasn't, "If you pray . . ." In Luke's Gospel Jesus taught his to disciples to, "pray always, and not lose heart" (Luke 18:1). To follow Jesus means we actively learn how to pray and build our lives around prayer.

The semantics of prayer confuse many. For some, the only experience with prayer is when they prayed at bedtime as a child, "Now I lay me down to sleep, I pray the Lord my soul to keep . . ." While touching and intimate, it doesn't match the complexities of our adult lives. When adults are lacking in their prayer life, I found it is from not knowing what to do or how to do it.

Jesus taught a very clear pattern. He said, "Go into your room and shut the door and pray to your father who is in secret; and your father who sees in secret will reward you" (Matthew 6:6). Notice that the place to start is with an intimate relationship with your heavenly Poppa, Pop, or Dad. For some calling God, "Dad" or "Father" is a stumbling block based on the negative experiences with their earthly father. For others, God or Father is a sexist term. I don't believe God gets too hung up on semantics. If you don't like calling God, "Father" then call God, "Mother." I could easily call God, "Mother" as my earthly mother is a powerful example of love, grace, and forgiveness. If calling God either father or mother is a hurdle, then use Yahweh, Jehovah, Ultimate Being, Creator of the Universe, or simply, "God." The important thing is that Jesus wants us to build a personal, intimate, and private relationship.

I teach people to find a place in their house that is "Their Place." It should be private and quiet. Make it a sanctuary, fill it with pictures, mementos, candles; anything sacred to you.

Now that you're quiet, what do you do? For Jesus, it was simple. Jesus said, "Do not heap up empty phrases . . ." Jesus wanted us to keep it simple. The prayer Jesus taught is a simple ten-line prayer, the Lord's Prayer—you pray in thirty seconds. For Jesus, it would be enough. I've tried just praying the Lord's Prayer and the ache in my soul is never satisfied. This is why I use a different form patterned after the Lord's Prayer; thanksgiving, supplication, intercession, praise, and dedication. But I still try to keep it simple.

Sometimes it is very difficult to quiet my brain. I go into my private sanctuary, close my eyes to pray, and suddenly my thoughts swirl like a tornado. Lately I've practiced Centering Prayer which is twenty minutes of quiet meditation. You choose one word that speaks to your heart. It could be peace, joy, Lord, Jesus; anything drawing you close to God. Close your eyes and focus on your breathing. Each time your mind wanders, gently repeat your word until your mind quiets. Sometimes in centering prayer, all I do is repeat my word. Lately I've used, "peace." Other times I find my brain quieting into the stillness where I hear God speak.

You can also choose a mantra for your prayer time. Followers of Jesus used mantras for centuries. Like the centering prayer, I encourage people to find words that are "their phrase." It must fit your soul like slipping on a glove. Some use the opening phrase of the Lord's Prayer, "Our Father (Mother, Ultimate Being), who art in heaven." Others use something like, "Let go and let God." Still others use the mantra that speaks to me, "Lord Jesus Christ, Son of God, have mercy on me." A mantra helps quiet my mind when I begin praying, I repeat it often throughout the day as a way of keeping myself close to God as I engage in my duties and tasks.

Many ask me about Eastern forms of meditation. I have practiced quiet meditation for years. If this form of spirituality speaks to your soul, then, do it. Silence of any kind is good. I find the primary difference between meditation and prayer is that while meditation takes us to silence, prayer is the next step as it allows us to listen for God's voice.

Does Prayer Work?

I love the question, "Does prayer work?" People are actually asking; Does God answer my prayers?" If they pray for their sick uncle or dying child, does God cure them? If they're unemployed and pray for a job, does God find them one? By reading what Jesus taught, you would think so. Jesus said, "So I tell you, whatever you ask for in prayer, believe that you have received it, and it will be yours (Mark 11:24). "Whatever you ask for in prayer, in faith, you will receive" (Matthew 21:22). I almost gave up on praying when, despite my prayers, a young man in my church died. It broke my heart.

He had an illness called Guillian Barre Syndrome. He was in his mid-twenties, a tremendous young man with his whole life in front of him. He caught the flu, recovered, but was then hospitalized with a kickback from the flu—Guillian Barre. He then slipped into a coma. Our congregation was traumatized. We held candlelight vigils, and also gathered the church leaders to pray. As minister, I quoted passages from Mathew, Mark, Luke, and Paul. I fervently asked God to grant our prayers and cure our friend. I believed in my heart; I had faith God heard our prayers. God didn't. Our young friend died after two weeks in a coma. After his funeral, I remember driving home and said to God,

"Screw you."

I was angry with God. There's no gentle way of saying it. I was hacked, betrayed and let down. I wanted to tear up the Bible again. Jesus had said all we had to do was ask in faith and our requests would be granted. Well, I prayed my brains out. I did everything the holy, revealed by God, inspired, interpreted, authoritative Bible said I should, and he still died. He hasn't been the only one over the years. Several others I prayed for also died. I began to think there was something wrong with me, my prayers were somehow defective, or I didn't have enough faith, or maybe I was asking in the wrong manner. I too began to wonder if prayer worked. However, as I kept at it, I realized my rants and tirades against God were also prayers. I found comfort knowing that there is a whole book of the Bible dedicated to being angry with God, Lamentations. There are many who wouldn't be following Jesus if it weren't for Lamentations. The pages of

Lamentations sum up all the pain, anger, betrayal, and abandonment of every follower of God. After my friend died, the best thing I did was stand up before God and shout lamentations at the top of my spiritual lungs. Now, granted I was in the basement, standing in the shower, but it still felt good to shout and shake my fist at God. To my surprise, God took it. It was OK to rant at God. It was expected and accepted as sacred and holy prayer. Ranting helped me trust God again. If I could trust God with my anger, then maybe I could trust God with my pain.

As I prayed over the years for those who died, there are some who lived. I've seen what I call medical miracles. I've seen people who were knocking at death's door suddenly revived. I've seen those who've prayed for jobs have them drop out of the sky. There doesn't seem to be any rhyme or reason. To be honest, sometimes I'm just baffled.

I've resolved myself to the great mystery of life and prayer; there's a tension I'll never resolve and was never intended to resolve. I don't know why Jesus said what he did about asking and it would be granted to us because it's not the case. Some facts of life can't be ignored. We're all going to die. Everyone who received a miraculous cure eventually died of something else. Crazy accidents happen in life leaving people maimed. There are birth defects that can't be cured. Diseases descend on people stripping them of life and then killing them. In each of these situations devout, faithful followers of Jesus got on their knees making their requests known to God. Sometimes prayers are answered, other times not. I've learned that, "No" is a perfectly good answer as well as, "maybe, not yet, someday, you're not ready, they're not ready, trust me, have faith." With prayer, I've learned to go beyond my request and simply trust God's Will. I follow Jesus's prayer in Gethsemane, "Not my will, but your will be done." Ultimately prayer is a great mystery leaving me humble. The humility brings wisdom and the wisdom teaches me there is something far greater at work.

In response to this mystery I've learned to pray in a different way. I begin by knowing that my heavenly Momma is God and I'm not. It's an important distinction that I often blur. Jesus said that our Ultimate Being knows our every need before we ask, (Matthew 6:8). This may lead some to wonder why we bother to pray at all, but with these prayers I know that Yahweh is aware of my life and my needs. When I pray, I approach God from the perspective God knows best for a particular situation.

Today I don't pray for cures. While I understand the human desire for our loved ones to be cured, it's often not in the divine books. I've learned that death is a transition to God, not a tragedy. Instead I pray for healing, the ultimate goal of God. I've seen those who were cured of an illness, but had a busted up, deader than a doornail soul. I've also witnessed those who have died of diseases do so with peace because their souls were healed. While curing is a medical process, healing is a spiritual one. I don't know a lot about medicine, but I do know about the spiritual processes. While medicine does not always heal a body, I know a soul can always be healed through prayer, scripture, contemplation, community, and if need be, therapy.

I stay away from prayers looking for concrete results. I pray for such things as wisdom, insight, guidance, clarity, and patience. I pray that I may be aware of God's presence in difficult and painful situations. I pray that I am willing to submit to God's Will in a particular situation. I pray that God will be God, that I will be God's child, and have the courage to accept her answer even if it is silence, pain, or death.

When I pray, I go back to the image that came to me in the mediation I shared earlier. God slung me over the divine shoulders. He knew the way through the weeds and my job was just to hang on. Perhaps the most appropriate prayer in the world is, "Oh Lord, help me hold on, if I fall, please catch me, if I hit the dirt, don't leave me behind, if I find myself behind, help me have the courage to find your way."

God Give Me the Lotto Numbers

The first time I thought prayer was shifty was in a football huddle in high school. Our coach gathered us in the end zone, made us all take a knee, and bow our heads. To this teenager, bowing in prayer during a football game just seemed odd, something even hypocritical. The coach started praying like a pastor before his congregation. He gripped the goal post like the edge of a pulpit and prayed that God would help us kick the butts of the other team. I remember opening one eye, raising an eyebrow, and wondering if God really cared who won a silly football game.

I've seen people pray for the craziest things. One time a woman told me she asked God to reveal the winning lotto numbers.

I kid you not.

She told me she prayed believing it had already happened. She bought the tickets as an act of faith. Puzzled when she didn't win, she told me she now doubted the power of prayer. In retrospect, were her prayers any different than my prayers for my young friend to be cured?

While leading worship one Sunday during the Iraq war, I prayed for those we call our enemies, that God would build bridges of understanding and peace. People were angry with the prayer. If I was a faithful American, I should be praying that our side should win. Kind of like a football game played on an international scale where God would help us kick their butts.

Praying in a restaurant seems to be a significant act of faith for many. They all join hands and bow their heads in a solemn show of devotion. Someone prays in a voice just loud enough to be heard at nearby tables asking God to sanctify their lives and bless their food. Why do they feel the need to do this? If they're asking God to bless their meal, then ok—I'll concede. But if they're trying to set an example to the heathens gathered at IHOP, then I think they're on shaky ground. They border on making a public display of their faith, something Jesus wasn't too fond of (Matthew 6:5).

So, what should we pray for? Are there things that are just flat out inappropriate? Yes, and no. While I believe God has numbered every hair on our heads, I don't believe God is too concerned with every wild spiritual hair that gets up our nose. We bother ourselves and God with things that just don't seem to make sense and aren't worth the worry. Having said this, God is willing to sit for hours listening to the daily concerns of our lives, hoping to earn our trust and hear our greatest burdens.

Blessed with three children, my wife and I love to listen to their chatter and share the details of their lives. If we want to build positive relationships with our children, we have to be open to everything on their minds. There are rewards when I am open and patient. If we're present in the little things, it earns us the right to be present in the big things. Because we sat with them through the years, day-by-day, listening to them and building relationships with them, we can talk with them about the big things in life. However, it is a challenge when an opportunity opens in the most unpredictable way. One day, driving with my teenage daughter, she unplugged her headphones and asked, "Dad, are Mormons Christian?" I almost swerved off the road. I didn't see that one coming. After years of patient listening to her chatting about the joys and challenges of being a teenager, it created a sacred space for her to share a deep spiritual question.

While shaving one morning my preteen son banged on the door and shouted, "Dad, hurry up, I have to talk to you! At my friend's youth group, the minister said if a kid isn't baptized in their church, they are going to hell. Is this true?" I nicked my nose with the razor. I didn't expect him to wrestle with heaven and hell at 7:30 in the morning. My son trusted me enough to spontaneously ask a nagging question.

I know this is the same with God. Paul says we are not to worry about anything, "But in prayer and supplication with thanksgiving, let your requests be made known to God" (Philippians 4:6). Like the good, perfect, heavenly Momma or Poppa, God wants to hear about all aspects of our lives.

So, if you want to pray for the lotto numbers . . . then pray for the numbers. If you must pray that your team wins, then go ahead and tell God to root for your team. If you need someone's butt kicked, I guess you can pray for that as well. It may raise a divine eyebrow but go ahead and pour it out.

During your time of prayer, pour out all the issues that seem overwhelming. List them, and then make check marks by the things God answers. But know in your heart that God is listening, is patient, and wants to do so much more. God is willing to listen to the little things, hoping at some point to earn the right to deal with the big things in your life.

Jesus said, "Seek first the kingdom of God and his righteousness" (Matthew 6:33). Jesus continues to point us beyond the little issues and towards the big issues. Jesus taught us to let go of worrying about food, shelter, and clothing, to focus on the weightier issues; forgiveness, pain, and suffering. Jesus knew that others would harm us and trespass over our physical, emotional, and spiritual boundaries. He knew our lives would be full of spiritual bile if we didn't learn to forgive those who trespassed against us. This is why Jesus taught that the central discipline of prayer was forgiveness and praying for our enemies. I had to learn how to pray for my enemies.

Pray for My Enemies

I had my identity stolen when someone broke into my car during a worship service. He took my wallet and checkbook. Call me stupid, but I left them in my car thinking, "Nobody would break into a car parked in a church parking lot." Right? Wrong. My life was a financial hell for the next year as the thief wrote checks and opened false bank accounts, all in my name. I was arrested for a crime he committed. Handcuffed, stripped searched, and wearing an orange jump suit, I spent a long night in jail because of his crime. I found myself stewing in my own private hate for the person who did this to me.

One afternoon an elderly woman in my congregation came to see me. She told me God sent her and she had a message for me. She said, "Steve, you must pray for your enemies and forgive. It is the only way."

God saw the depths of my soul and how my anger was tearing me up. God and the woman were right. It was time to forgive and let go. It wasn't murder or rape; it was just a chaotic mess. Each check written caused deeper financial chaos—I had to intentionally pray for my unknown enemy. I had to pray for his trespasses because I knew God forgave me my trespasses. Slowly over the year, I came to believe that my identity was stolen to teach me a deeper aspect of prayer. It's one thing to teach about praying for an enemy, it is another thing to pray for someone who harmed you. Through praying for forgiveness, I could let go of the hate, resentment, and frustration, and focus instead on God's blessing and grace. I felt God was building a bridge of prayer between this person and myself. Eventually, through prayer, I found peace again in my life. It may be one of the most profound aspects of following this Jesus Path. Instead of allowing those who harm us to create anger and resentment, we pray for our enemies to let go of the hatred and pain and find as Paul said, "A peace that passes understanding" (Philippians 4:7).

Pray without Ceasing

Following the Jesus Path of Prayer is a daily, life-long journey weaving the other paths together. Paul said, "Rejoice always, pray without ceasing, give thanks in all circumstances; for this is the Will of God in Christ Jesus for you." (1 Thessalonians 5:16-18).

We began the Jesus Path with joy, "Rejoice always." We allow the joy of Christ to fill us. When our lives are filled with joy it leads us to "Pray without ceasing." As we practice prayer it becomes part of our daily existence, teaching us that all of life is sacred.

"Give thanks in all circumstances." In the Path of God's Will we know God is present, working to bring us to a place of hope and joy.

"For this is the Will of God." When we contemplate God's Will for our lives, we learn that prayer is God's highest priority. Prayer teaches us that we are never separated from God. Despite sin, pain, or brokenness, God is with us and through prayer we are with God.

"In Christ Jesus for you." Prayer is a gift to us from Christ Jesus. It teaches us the most profound aspects of life: forgiveness, love, and peace (1 Thessalonians 5:18).

May it Not Be Forever

One time while praying, I heard my father's voice say, "May it not be forever." It made me smile. He had been gone for over a year, yet he was there, alive in my heart and soul. I took his words as a promise. The imprint he left many years ago will be fulfilled in an embrace. At some point, in some way, in the paradise of resurrection, we will greet one another and experience a divine oneness. I believe it will be the same way with God. When we enter the gates of paradise, there will come the voice of the divine Poppa, the holy Momma, welcoming us into the resurrection. We will be with God, we will be at home.

Chapter Nine: The Path

of Managing the Shadow

It was out of my mouth in a flash. I cursed the soul of a man I was working with. He was a total pain. It was bad enough that I cursed him, but I cursed him in the presence of another parishioner as well. Their shocked expressions were instantaneous. It wasn't that I cursed, but I stepped over the line, I cursed another man's soul. I was tired, he had tested my patience for months, and had pushed me too far. I had enough and just wanted to be done with him. Yet, he was a member of my church and my responsibility was to constantly care for him. I failed my calling. It was more than losing my patience; it reflected something deeper.

This is just the beginning of my issues. I had problems in my life I didn't want to talk about. I hated admitting they were there, and if people knew about them they'd want nothing to do with me. I only shared this darkness with my wife, my therapist, and God. For better or worse I've also learned this darkness binds us together. We all have something we carry around like a spiritual bag of rocks. Even those who claim they're enlightened drag this baggage around.

We're messy creations. We're a contradiction in terms; we are fully divine, and are one with Jesus, and one with God. I believe we have the ability to fully embody the divine essence in our lives. Yet, things pick and nag at us. Jesus says the kingdom of God is within us. But my rejoinder to that is then the kingdom of God is a mess.

Followers of Jesus must admit we cast a long shadow. I use Carl Jung's term, *shadow*, as it accurately describes our spiritual condition. The Christian tradition has another word for it; sin.

Many followers of Jesus don't like to use the term Sin. It feels archaic and judgmental. We'd like to ditch this term from our spiritual lexicon along with any other term begging spiritual flagellation. But it is a helpful term.

The Greek word for sin is "hamartia," from the world of archery meaning "missing the mark." Just as an archer aims, shoots, and misses the bull's eye, so we miss the mark. We have good intentions, but just when we think we've nailed it, something happens, and things go awry. We trip over our ego, we're proud of our humility, we're frustrated that others don't appreciate our effort, we miss the mark, we sin.

If we were only missing the mark, I'd feel ok. I just need to practice, and I'll eventually improve. However, in my life, hamartia is more than just missing the bull's eye; it is describing a more profound problem.

Sin is a skid mark on our soul. It's dark goo. The more we try to remove it from our lives the more we get mired in its mess. The church traditions described the root of the sin problem by calling them the Seven Deadly Sins; envy, gluttony, greed, lust, pride, sloth, and wrath. When left unaddressed, these attributes not only destroy us, but those around us.

However, all is not lost. If you're going to follow Jesus, you must learn to manage your shadow. Just because the goo is pervasive doesn't mean it is destructive. Actually, once understood, sin is a great asset allowing our divinity to shine. It's a tension in our faith. Sin takes us to a deeper understanding of who we are as God's divine creation.

Drawing Close to God

To manage our shadow, we first must realize that our sin draws us closer to God. Paul had to learn this lesson. Though he was a spiritual hero, he had to come to terms with what he called, "A thorn in the flesh"

(2 Corinthians 12:7). Paul described something in his life that was a skid mark, goo, a burr under the saddle, a thorn. It embarrassed him and brought him to his knees. Like us, I imagine Paul felt that if people knew about his thorn they wouldn't want him to be a church leader. He asked God three times to remove it from him. And each time God said, "My grace is sufficient for you. My power is made perfect through your weakness" (2 Corinthians 12:9). This verse guides us as we practice this path.

Sin is present in our lives to draw us close to God. Like that sharp pain of a splinter under my fingernail, I feel that spiritual ache I described in the chapter on prayer. I desire to stretch out before God and admit that I'm a loser. However, I hear God say instead I'm not a lost cause; I'm a child of God. God's grace shines like a brilliant light on my shadow and I feel a divine radiant glow. Instead of damning my soul, sin allows the grace of the Ultimate Holy One to shine. I feel God pick me up, dust me off, and whisper in my ear, "You are loved, you are beautiful, you are perfect just the way you were created." This is the first step in managing the shadow. Instead of sin being a plague on our lives, it ultimately reminds us of our divinity. Sin is a pervasive darkness only when we refuse to acknowledge its presence. The more we deny it, the more it controls us. When we allow the pain of sin to draw us close to God, it allows God to remind us of our true divinity.

The second step of managing the shadow is to constantly learn that God's power is made perfect through our weakness. As we draw near to God and realize God's grace, the danger is to puff ourselves up and take the claim for God's power. We manage our shadow by learning that we don't shine the divine light in the world, but we magnify God's love and power. As a prism depends on an outside source of light to create a rainbow, so are we dependent on God's light. When we draw close to God through our weakness, God's brilliance shines through us. We begin to realize it's not us working in the world, but it's God's power working through us. God's power is made perfect through our weakness. For me, it's all about humility.

Humility is one of the hardest lessons I've had to learn. One Sunday afternoon as I was leaving church, I was excited, I had nailed the sermon. "Damn you're good. You're Mister Silver Tongue. People were eating out of the palm of your hand. They ate up every word you spoke." I opened the car door, threw my briefcase in the backseat, and stooped to enter the car. Then I banged the side of my head on the roof of the car. I didn't bump my head because I narrowly missed the entrance; no, I banged the side of my head. If you were watching me, you might think I had never sat in a car before. As the stars twinkled in my brain, I heard this distinct divine laughter, "Damn, you're good, so good you can't even get your fat head through the car door." I needed to learn that my spiritual gift of preaching was getting in the way of God working. Others thought, as did I, that I was the great preacher. But God's divine light was stifled. I had to learn that God's power is made perfect through me. I had to learn how to do the divine duck.

The Divine Duck

We do the divine duck when we get out of God's way. We realize it's not about us, but about God's light and God's power shining through us. We must learn how to duck so God can work. This is one of the reasons why I have a hard time with the concept of, "making a difference."

It's one of the most common terms we use to find meaning and purpose in life. People say, "You have to make a difference. You will find significance when you make a difference in someone's life." This seems true on the surface. Self-sacrifice on behalf of others feels good. But it is also when the goo of the soul seeps out and taints our actions.

Before long we are proud of what we're doing. *We're* making a difference. When you think *you* made the difference you've missed the mark. Ultimately you can't make a difference. You are in the way of something bigger. God is the only entity that truly makes a difference in people's lives. It is God who is powerful; it is God who is transformative. God's power shines through us and our purpose is to magnify that power towards others. It's a matter of intention. If it's all about us, then that's truly all it is, us.

But when we act and then duck, to get out of the way, then we're the prisms where God's presence sparkles through. As we manage the shadow we learn to get out of God's way so God can shine.

Evil

To manage the shadow, we need to learn how to call a spade a spade. We need to learn how to name what is evil.[1] Many who follow Jesus don't like to talk about evil. Like the term sin, we hate to call something or someone evil. For some it is a dated term. In our day of psychology and psychiatry, we'd rather call negative actions "interpersonal dysfunctions," or some behavior category from the DSM (*Diagnostic, and Statistical Manuel of Mental Disorders*). We call someone who kills, a murderer, someone who robs, a thief, or someone who sexually violates another person, a perpetrator. But to manage our shadow we need to step across a boundary and call the negative actions that people commit as "evil." The reason why it's necessary to name negative and violent actions as evil is to avoid committing evil ourselves, and instead commit ourselves to living positively in the world.

---

[1] Many of my thoughts about Evil are found in my previous book, *Sent to Soar*, Quest Books, 2014.

E-V-I-L and L-I-V-E

The two counter forces in our world are a force for God, and a force against God. Scott Peck in his book, *People of the Lie* (New York: Simon and Schuster, 1983) describes it perfectly. There is a force for l-i-v-e, which is a force for God. The counter force in the creation is e-v-i-l. It is live spelled backward. If life's complexities could be drawn as a linear line with l-i-v-e on one side and e-v-i-l on the other, and we stand in the middle; the free will that God gave us allows us day-by-day to step either towards l-i-v-e or e-v-i-l. While I believe there are gray areas in our lives, I also believe that with evil it's an either/or. When we don't manage our shadow, we're not self-reflected, or do not understand our darkness, our sin, our brokenness, we can slip and slide towards evil and destruction in our lives. However, the converse is also true. If we self-reflect, allow our sin to draw us close to God, and get out of God's way, then we work towards life.

Those who follow Jesus seek to constantly manage the messy side of their lives to work towards life. Jesus teaches several ways to do this; return no person evil for evil, pray for your enemies, and love one another. Those who follow the path of Jesus are committed to making the hard decisions for life—and they are hard decisions. You might not be someone who murders someone, but Jesus said that even if you are angry with someone you committed a grievous act just as significant. Jesus says it this way, "You have heard that it is said of those of ancient times, 'You shall not murder and whoever murders shall be liable to judgment.' But I say to you that if you are angry with a brother or sister, you will be liable to judgment, and if you insult a brother or sister you will be liable to the council, and if you say, 'You fool,' you will be liable to the hell of fire (Matthew 5:21-22). You may never have sex with someone outside of your marriage but if you, "look at a woman (man) with lust you have already committed adultery with them in your heart

(5:28). He does the same with divorce (5:31, 32), swearing (5:33, 34), vengeance (5:38-42) and love of neighbor and enemy (5:43-47). Jesus takes our concepts of violent actions and expands them until we are guilty. This is why we manage our shadow because we unwittingly participate and can unleash a negative, if not violent tide.

Sin has an exponential component. When we participate in sin on any level, we release a tide that sweeps others into a negative vortex that encourages them to act in evil ways. You flip me off on the freeway, I flip you off back. It doesn't sound like much in the grand scheme of moral ethics, but at what point does it escalate to road rage?

Sin has a mob mentality. Just as a riot sucks innocent bystanders into committing acts of violence, so does evil. Others cheat on their taxes and get away with it, so why don't you do so as well. At what point are thousands cheating on taxes because others have done the same? Is it stealing to cheat on taxes? Is it on the same ethical scale as grand larceny? Jesus would say it is. We commit ourselves to life because of this.

Life also releases an exponential energy. My wife was driving in the community the other day. When she came to an intersection, she saw a man in a wheel chair stuck in the intersection. Other drivers were whizzing by, some honking their horns. She pulled her car over, went out into the intersection, and asked the man if he needed help. He said that yes, he was stuck. As she pushed his wheel chair out of the intersection, suddenly others stopped and asked if they could be of assistance. Because she was willing to act in a generous way, she unleashed an infectious energy. Her actions invited others to do the same. Jesus taught the parable of the Good Samaritan as an example of this. It's a story of a person going out of his way to help someone who was mugged and left by the side of the road. Religious people crossed to the other side and passed the man by. However, a Samaritan (a citizen of a foreign land) stopped to help the man, even paying for his medical aid (Luke 10:25-37). Jesus said we must all act this way as we unleash a tide of goodness. We help build the kingdom of God by our sacrificial actions, but we also encourage others to do the same. Through our actions, we unleash life.

Baby Steps

The average moral person rarely commits an evil act. If someone commits something opposed to their morals, they're usually horrified at what they've done. They're filled with remorse, grief, and shame. They want to fall on their knees before God and before others, seeking forgiveness. It's easily corrected by confrontation, confession, reflection, and redirection.

What's frightening is when someone does not manage their shadow and commits evil as a normal course of their life. With a piece at a time they compromise themselves to the point where the sin and evil they do is just part of their daily lives.

Tom had incredible musical gifts. People traveled for miles to hear him play the piano and organ. The choir grew as singers were inspired by his abilities. However, Tom was a pathological liar. He undermined the credibility and reputation of others by spreading false rumors of alcohol addiction and illicit affairs. He smeared people's integrity with his dark allegations. He was a contradiction. On the one hand, he was a brilliant musician and claimed to follow Jesus. On the other hand, he had a pervasive shadow and darkness. With each lie or false rumor Tom baby stepped into evil. His allegations left destruction in his wake.

Was Tom a murderer? Did he commit grand larceny? No, but he sinned. He missed the mark. His actions were evil. His sin consumed him. He was sucked into a vortex that destroyed people's lives.

As followers of Jesus we need to work at managing our shadows. It keeps us from slipping into destructive life patterns that create evil.

As we manage the evil in our lives many followers of Jesus question the presence of the Devil. Some wonder if he is the author of this evil. They worry that this entity lures them down the slippery slope towards destruction. If we are to manage our shadow, do we need to manage the presence of an evil one, and if so, how do we do this?

The Devil

When some followers of Jesus talk about sin and evil they often talk about the Devil. The Devil goes by many names; Satan, the Adversary, Beelzebub, and Old Scratch. Many followers of Jesus are divided on the existence of a devil. Many insist there's a devil who is an entity outside of us luring us down the path of evil. They believe the devil is a fallen angel, someone who stands opposed to God and God's goodness. This entity is also the ruler of hell, the dwelling place of damned souls.

Other followers of Jesus say there isn't a devil, but it is a by-product from the Roman oppression at the end of the first century. They understand the devil as a metaphor for the power of evil in our lives.

Did Jesus believe in a devil? According to the gospels Jesus did believe. In Matthew's Gospel, the Devil tempted him in the wilderness. He taught that those who did not show compassion would be cast into "eternal fire prepared for the devil and his angels." When the seventy people he sent on a mission journey came back to share what they had done, he was overjoyed at the power they experienced and said, "I watched Satan fall from heaven like a flash of lightning" (Luke 10:18). Satan is referenced in all the gospels—Jesus was opposed to a figure he called either Satan, the Devil, or Beelzebub, who caused evil and sin in the world. Did Jesus really deal with this Satan, or is he the product of the oppression at the end of the first century?

I do not believe in a literal devil. As described in the Path of the Bible, I take the Bible seriously, not literally. I interpret the Bible considering historical events. I believe the Bible's authors, writing seventy years after Jesus's resurrection, experienced intense oppression by the Roman armies. As they sought to understand their oppressors, they borrowed stories and images from what we refer to as Jewish Apocalypticism. These images were filled with a destructive being they described as their Roman oppressors. These images were written into the stories of Jesus to show that God was working for them, against their oppressors.

Some followers of Jesus say I pick and choose which parts of the Bible to believe and which to reject. That is not the case—I'm choosing to interpret the Bible through historical lenses. By taking the Bible seriously, I'm freed from worrying about a demonic entity who stands apart from God and seeks to destroy humanity. Instead of fighting against a devil, it allows me to understand Satan as a metaphor for the destructive power of evil. Just as Jesus was tempted by the Devil, so we are tempted to slide down the slope of evil. Just as Jesus saw the Devil fall from the sky like a bolt of lightning, so we break the power of evil when striving for life. The metaphor of the Devil helps me manage my shadow. It shows the power of unchecked sin in my life. If I don't allow my sin to draw me closer to God, then my sin draws me closer to an evil power. If I'm not doing the divine duck to allow God's light to shine through me, then I have the potential to spread darkness.

It's one of the central paths of following Jesus. As children of God we shine God's light to the world. We radiate the love of God and we do this in part by managing the potential for darkness in our lives. We name evil and then step towards life. We know that the darkness has the power to destroy our lives and those around us. We follow Jesus by managing our shadow.

Did Jesus Die for My Sins?

A common statement that followers of Jesus make is that Jesus "died for our sins." Paul said that Jesus died for our sins so that we could be led to eternal life (Romans 5:25). We need to understand this and other verses in the context they were written and then apply them to our lives.

We need to remember that the New Testament authors lived in a sacrificial culture. To have your sins forgiven an animal needed to be sacrificed for those sins. As these first-century followers of Jesus began to understand the effect of Jesus on their lives, they saw Jesus's death as the perfect sacrifice, so perfect they no longer needed to sacrifice animals. Jesus's death freed them from the burden of their sins.

The key here is "freed." Personally, I don't believe that Jesus was sacrificed by God to free us or forgive us from our sins. If God is all-powerful and all-loving, why couldn't God simply forgive us? Why did God require a blood sacrifice?

For some, the belief that Jesus died for their sins is the bedrock of their faith. To be a Christian one had to accept that Jesus died for their sins. It frees them, and I think they have the right to believe this. They take the Bible verses and this concept literally. Following Jesus gives them permission to believe this way.

Others need to believe that Jesus died for their sins because of the large burden of guilt they carry. They committed some type of crime, literal, spiritual, or otherwise. Believing that Jesus died to take away these sins frees them from this burden. I also think these people have the permission, and the need, to believe that Jesus did this for them.

I could never accept or comprehend that Jesus died for my sins. It took me years to understand I could believe differently about Jesus, could still follow him, and could call myself a Christian. When I realized there was a new way to understanding Jesus's death, it brought me to the Path of Joy—it freed me.

To understand Jesus as he relates to our sins, I take the Bible seriously, not literally. I understand the context of the passage. The first followers of Jesus sacrificed animals as a way of feeling free from their sins. For them, seeing Jesus as the perfect sacrifice freed them. They never had to sacrifice again. Just as the blood of a sacrificed animal cleansed them from their sin, so did the blood that poured out from Jesus body at the time of his death cleanse them. I understand how freeing this perspective was for them.

It's not for me.

I do not live in a sacrificial culture. We don't sacrifice things to feel God's forgiveness. Jesus died because of what he stood for. He had a vision of God's love for people he was willing to die for. I embrace this vision of following Jesus and it frees me. I'm free from legalisms. I can accept how others, whether they are first century Christians, evangelical Christians, or any other brand of the thirty-three thousand denominations, understand the effect that Jesus's death and resurrection had on their lives and I freely disagree with them. Again, the key is freedom. Jesus sets us free. As Paul said in his letter to the Galatians, Christ has set us free (Galatians 5:1). Jesus set me free from the burden of my sins.

Instead of carrying the guilt of my sins, I discovered the grace and love of God. The meaning of Jesus's death was freedom. Jesus set us free from the burden of our sins whether we take the Bible literally or seriously. Instead of requiring the blood of Jesus to wipe away my sins, I feel God's love embrace me. My sin sends me into the arms of God where God wraps me like a mother's hug. God's compassion flows over me. Through God's love I know my sins are forgiven and I have a new start in my life. Through Jesus's life and God's presence I experience joy. There's that word again, joy. Jesus came to bring us joy. Through my sins, I experience joy because I know God has forgiven me.

Our sins, our shadows, do not need to ultimately destroy our lives. If we manage our actions, our motives and intentions, how we speak to others and how we listen to them and respond, then our shadow ultimately brings in light. The mystic, Julian of Norwich, had a vision where Jesus said to her, "All will be well, and all will be made well." Jesus told her that we needed to trust in the wisdom and power of God. Even in the face of evil, God ultimately redeems the evil and the person who commits evil, and all will be made well.

Our shadow is the place of great learning. We find grace from the ragged edge of our souls, and we're drawn into God's love. It's the place where we can identify the pain of others and work towards healing. Henri Nouwen in his book, *The Wounded Healer* (Double Day. 1972), described that our sin and pain allow us to be a wounded healer. Through our pain, we're able to identify with another's pain. We're able to minister to others not from our strength, but through our wounds. It's God's word to Paul, "My power is made perfect through your weakness."

The former alcoholic can minister to another alcoholic because she's walked that path. The same goes for the former drug addict ministering to those battling addictions. And those who have struggled with depression, mental illness, or spiritual dryness can minister to those facing the same struggles. A wounded healer is someone dealing with arrogance, pride, or other shadows standing in the way of spiritual fullness. We manage our shadow when we minister to others out of the pain we deal with in our own lives.

All Shall Be Made Well

Our shadows, while prevalent in our lives, do not need to be destructive. If we manage our shadow, if we are self-reflective, understand our actions, and seek to hit the mark, we draw close to God's grace and light. While we may plead with God to never allow us to sin again, we need to remember that ultimately, this sin is never removed from us. Like an alcoholic always in a state of recovery, so are we always in a state of recovering from our sin. However, it is through this thorn in our flesh, our sin, that God's power is made perfect in the world. If we're able to get out of God's way, then God's light shines through our weakness. Through our weakness, we draw close to others and seek to heal their wounds.

Where do you sin in your life? What do you hide from others in shame? What is your shadow? When we travel the Jesus Path we know that ultimately God can heal us and "All shall be made well."

Chapter Ten: The Path of Resurrection

People face death in two ways. Some struggle with it. Standing on the brink of their passing, they push, fight, and try with all their might to stay alive until the power of death overcomes them. They are like Jan who tried one chemo treatment after another looking for the magic cocktail to extend her life by a few short months. She had a limited quality of life in her final days. She was nauseated and weak, with sores filling her mouth. She fought against death until there were no other options. The process of dying overcame her will to live, and she finally died, never finding tranquility or acceptance.

Others die peacefully. They don't struggle or fight against it, they calmly accept the end of their life. As the power of the dying process overcomes them, they let go with love and accept what comes next. They are like Alex who lived with a brain tumor for seven years. He stood on the brink of death several times; then the tumor would shrink again. He knew the tumor could expand at any moment and he would die. Yet unlike Jan, Alex traveled the road of joy. He was guided by his north star. He reached out to those suffering from cancer by modeling hope and courage. He knew death was inevitable as the tumor began to expand, but he was not discouraged. He was gracious to his doctors and nurses. He accepted his family's love. When Alex and I talked on several occasions about death and dying, he was not afraid. As he entered hospice, Alex was at peace. He held his parents' hands and simply let go.

What were the differences between Jan and Alex? What causes one to struggle and the other to calmly accept the process of dying? Will I be like Jan or Alex? I believe the difference is an understanding of the resurrection. Jan thought her life was over. It had come to an end, and dirt was the only thing awaiting her. Alex believed his death was merely a transition. A complete transformation awaited Alex. His body would die, but his soul would be released. His soul, his uniqueness, that which made him, "Alex" would continue. At the moment of his death, Alex would enter the resurrection—paradise.

The resurrection is one of the key Jesus paths. It is the summation of Jesus's teachings. It is the promise Jesus held out to each of us. We are transformed in death, and its power transforms how we live as well.

The concept of resurrection is confusing. There are many different beliefs about the resurrection. As I share my understanding of the resurrection, I hope its power inspires you in life as well as how you anticipate your death.

Lazarus

There is a story from John's Gospel about the death of Lazarus, one of Jesus's friends. Jesus heard of Lazarus's death when traveling in the countryside and when he arrived at Lazarus's home, he had been dead for three days. Lazarus's sisters were filled with both anguish and hope; the anguish that they had lost their brother, and the hope that Jesus would bring their brother back from the dead. When the sisters questioned Jesus, he said to them, "I am the resurrection and the life. Those who believe in me, even though they die, will live, and everyone who lives and believes in me will never die" (John 11:17). Jesus then yelled into Lazarus's tomb, "Come out!" And Lazarus came back to life. He walked out of the tomb draped in his grave clothes. Jesus said, "Unbind him and let him go."

The story of Lazarus begs the question of resurrection. Is this the resurrection? Does resurrection mean our bodies will come back to life as did Lazarus? Is this what awaits us? Some followers of Jesus believe this is true, however, I don't. Instead, I take this story as a metaphor needing to be interpreted. I believe the story means that the power that brought Lazarus back to life is symbolic of a power that transforms our living and our dying.

How does this power relate to Jesus's death and resurrection?

Jesus's Resurrection

Jesus's resurrection is the model of what happens to all of us. Each gospel story has a different account of what happened. But the basic story is that after Jesus died, his disciples laid him in a large tomb. They rolled a stone in front of the opening, sealing Jesus inside. Women came to anoint Jesus's body with spices three days later. They wondered how they would roll the stone away, but as they approached, they found the stone had already been moved. The women looked inside and saw an angel who said, "Do not be afraid, for I know that you are looking for Jesus, who was crucified. He is not here; he has risen, just as he said" (Matthew 28:5-6).

From this point, the stories differ. John's gospel describes that Mary goes back to the disciples to tell them what she saw. Peter and another disciple run to the tomb and finding it empty, return home. Mary returns to the tomb and stands at the entrance weeping. The resurrected Jesus comes to her and says, "Woman, why are you weeping?" (John 20:13) Mary does not recognize Jesus and thinks he is the gardener. She asks him where they have taken the body of Jesus. Jesus then says Mary's name, and suddenly she recognizes him. She clings to Jesus, but he says, "Do not hold on to me, for I have not ascended to the Father" (vs 17).

Luke, Matthew, and John each tell of the resurrected Jesus appearing to the disciples several times. Sometimes he appeared as a ghost-like apparition before the disciples in locked rooms or along roadways. Other times Jesus was a physical being where he ate a meal and invited the disciples to touch his body and wounds. The resurrection poses many questions leading followers of Jesus to have different beliefs about its meaning and how it applies to their lives.

Some believe that Jesus physically rose from the dead. Like Lazarus, they believe God miraculously resuscitated and transformed Jesus's body into a living being. For these followers, it is the hallmark of their faith; the core reason why they follow Jesus.

Other followers of Jesus believe his resurrection was a spiritual experience. They see the resurrection stories as examples of God's power to transform our life and death. For these people, Jesus's body didn't need to be physically resurrected to have significance. They do not take the stories of Jesus's resurrection literally, but seriously.

After years of thought, contemplation, conversation, and meditation, I believe the resurrection was a spiritual experience. I do not believe Jesus's body physically resuscitated from the dead. I understand the stories of Jesus's resurrection to be symbolic. My understanding isn't less significant than those who take it literally. For both sides, it's important to understand that Jesus's resurrection is a cornerstone of our faith.

What does it mean to have a spiritual understanding of the resurrection? Through this spiritual understanding, I find a sense of God's meaning, power, and peace, which is the key insight of the resurrection. This spiritual understanding of the resurrection transformed my faith and life.

Every aspect of the resurrection points to the great truth of God's power. Jesus in the tomb was symbolic of the death experience we all face. Just as the women mourned when they anointed Jesus's body with spices, we carry a similar grief knowing our death is final. God rolled the stone away showing God's power to roll away any stones holding us back, sealing us in, and suffocating us.

When the angel speaks to the women, it reflects the mystical ways that God speaks to us. The empty tomb represents a new beginning in our lives. Jesus's renewed body shows that God can transform our lives into something new. Jesus's life beyond death models how God breaks the chains of death, ushering us into eternal life. When Jesus appeared to the disciples after his resurrection, it is how Jesus appears to us. Sometimes Jesus appears to us in mysterious ways. He comes to us when we least expect it. These spiritual experiences are so real it's as if we can touch his body and feel his wounds.

Resurrection means that life is more than a humdrum, day-to-day existence. God transforms and resurrects us, so every day we can practice and live the Jesus Path. Meaning is found in every aspect of our lives, through relationships with significant people; friends, people in our community, spouses, children, and extended family. Resurrection takes our daily grind and transforms it into something meaningful.

Through the resurrection, we discover God's power in life and death. God's power moves through our lives like the force of a stream in the Path of God's Will. God's power overcomes the obstacles we face. God's power changes the tragedy of death into a time of spiritual transition.

The resurrection brings peace. I know God is with us through the trials and challenges we face daily. As with Alex, the resurrection brings us peace knowing that just as God is with us in life, God is with us in death. We have peace believing that as God broke the chains of Jesus's death, so God breaks the chains of our death and ushers us into a paradise that is dramatic, majestic, and profound.

Following the Path of Resurrection requires practice. We practice this when we have faith that God resurrects our lives and gives us unflagging hope. Despite the circumstances, good or bad, we do not stop hoping, because as it says in the old folk hymn, *we shall overcome, someday.*

We practice the resurrection when we act in our lives. We must engage the challenges we face. If God is working in our lives, then we must work as well. We need to be creative, using our gifts and resources to solve problems with viable solutions.

We practice the Path of Resurrection when we endure. As the philosopher, Teilhard de Chardin said, "Above all, trust in the slow work of God," (from his poem, *Patient Trust*). God's resurrection hope often takes a lifetime to fulfill, but it always overcomes darkness, pain, or evil.

The resurrection moves in two directions in our lives. Just as we experience meaning, power, and peace in our lives, so we experience these qualities in our death.

Where's the Hope?

When teaching the resurrection from a spiritual and symbolic perspective, many feel I've ripped the rug out from under them. If Jesus didn't physically rise from the dead, if his body wasn't resuscitated, then what does it mean for them and their death? Like Jan who knew she would cease to exist, will they just die and that's the end? Or does something else happen to us? Something we call heaven or eternal life?

Yes, there is!

Initially, the resurrection is physical—our bodies die. Then we are either cremated or buried. But if our bodies are not resuscitated and we don't physically rise from the dead, then what happens next?

Paul describes that we are raised as a spiritual body. When we are alive, we have a physical body with flesh and bones. When we die, our physical body is destroyed, and our spiritual body is raised (1 Corinthians 15:44). Our soul separates from our body and enters heaven and paradise.

Heaven

Lynn knew she was dying; it was a matter of days. We talked about heaven as she lay on her hospice bed. As her death drew near, she asked, "Where am I going after I die? What will it be like? Is it a garden full of flowers and butterflies?" Mitch asked me the same thing as he was in hospice, as did Beth, Jane, Mike, and countless others during my career as a pastor. People want to know what will happen to them after they die. They want to know about heaven.

I've not experienced the afterlife, so what I'm sharing is conjecture on my part. However, I've had visions, dreams, and images of what happens after we die. I have listened to and read about many people who had life-after-death experiences. Based on my knowledge and what others have told me I've tried to stitch together images of what happens to us. It may be conjecture on my part, but it's what I teach to those who wonder what's going to happen to them after they die. If you asked me on your deathbed about what happens after I die, I could say with all assurance, "We can trust our good and loving God to take care of us after we die." Some say I should just leave it at that. None of us knows with certainty what happens, so we should just have faith God will care for us. However, I believe we can know what this trust and faith in God looks like after we die.

What Happens Next

Jesus said, "Today, you will be with me in paradise." This phrase comes from a conversation with one of the two thieves who was crucified with Jesus. One thief derided Jesus; the other repented for his wrongdoing. He asked Jesus to "Remember me when you come into your kingdom." Jesus replied, "Today you will be with me in paradise" (Luke 23:42, 43). This lone sentence describes the spiritual dimensions of what happens after our bodies die.

Today

Jesus said, "Today." He taught that there is immediacy about what happens to us after we die. We don't wait; there is no span of time when we are separated from God. Whatever happens is instantaneous, right now, "today." Paul says it happens, "In a flash, in the twinkling of an eye" (1 Corinthians 15:52).

I've attended the death of several hundred people. On a few occasions, I was blessed to see the soul lift from the body as the person died. While this seems outrageous, several other pastors and hospice nurses told me they experienced the same thing.

I was in a hospital room as a family gathered around their father to say their goodbyes. We said prayers and waited for their loved one to die. In that final moment, the family's attention focused on their dying father. Just after he died, while his body was still lying on the hospital bed, I saw his soul sit up and lift in the air. Like Jesus, he had a physical quality, yet he was spiritual. His soul was shimmering, holy, and ethereal. While the family's focus was still on the dead body, the father's soul looked with curiosity at his family gathered around him. He then looked at me and turned towards the window in his room. He then walked through the window and was gone. What occurred was immediate; there was no waiting; it happened in a twinkling of an eye as Jesus said it happened, "Today."

You Will Be with Me

Jesus said, "Today *you* will be with me." What does this mean? Is the thief's body with Jesus? No, as I've said before, the thief's body dies. But the elements making the thief unique, something beyond his body, is preserved. I call this the thief's soul.

Our souls make us unique people. God gave us our soul at some point in our creation. Our body houses our soul which gives us personality. Our soul is filled with spiritual gifts and inspires and fills us with creativity. It connects us to God throughout our lives. When Jesus said to the thief, "you" will be with me, I believe Jesus refers to his soul, his unique identity. This is significant because our soul stays intact. Notice that Jesus does not say we will be dispersed into thousands of particles, but our soul is kept together. Our soul is not lost—it is preserved and at the moment of our death this unique spiritual essence releases from our body.

Then Jesus said to the thief, "you . . . will be with *me*." At that instant, we are not left alone; we are in the presence of something spiritual. Like Jesus, our body dies and our soul, our spiritual essence, goes forward. Jesus experienced the same resurrection as we do. "He" transformed into something new and divine. This divine spiritual essence of Jesus is with us after we die.

I find great comfort in this. I have followed Jesus my whole life. In my death, the Jesus I follow meets me and welcomes me to what's next. Since I entrusted Jesus with my life, I can trust Jesus to lead me to what's next.

This does not mean that you must follow Jesus in life to experience his essence after his death. We are meeting Jesus's divine essence, not his physical body. It could be that a Buddhist, a Hindu, or a Taoist, experiences something different after they die, but whatever it is, I believe it is divine. I even believe atheists will experience this divinity in some way, shape, or form. I believe this divine experience is universal and is granted to every human being. It may look different for everyone, but for me, I'll take Jesus's words and will meet his divine essence.

Paradise

Jesus said, *"Today you will be with me . . . in paradise."* What is "paradise?" Lynn wanted paradise to be a beautiful garden with flowers and butterflies. What do you want it to be? A Caribbean beach, a view from the top of a mountain peak, or a green fairway where your drive is always straight and perfect? Many people have glimpsed "paradise."

Don Piper's book *Ninety Minutes in Heaven: A True Story of Life and Death (Revel, 2004)* describes the paradise he saw after his car wreck killed him. Before he returned to his body, he saw colors he had never seen before and sounds beyond comprehension. Eben Alexander in his book *Proof of Heaven: A Neurosurgeons' Journey into the Afterlife (Simon and Schuster: 2012)* also described a paradise with vivid colors and sounds. He had a spirit guide who met and guided him. Each had different experiences, but there are significant similarities. After their deaths, what happened was immediate. They did not lose their uniqueness as individuals. They didn't feel alone and were surrounded by a holy presence. What they experienced was paradise.

I love that paradise is open for interpretation. If some believe in reincarnation, then paradise allows room for that definition. If some enter through beautiful gates into a celestial place, there is room for that as well. Maybe your description of paradise is a place where God lovingly accepts your soul and moves you into eternal life; then that too is paradise.

Jesus's phrase of *"Today you will be with me . . . in paradise"* has nothing to do with hell or damnation. He doesn't condemn one thief to hell and the other to paradise. When I teach this, many ask, "But what about those who have caused great pain and committed evil in their lives? What about the Hitlers, the Stalins, the murderers, and the rapists? Are they treated the same way as those of us who committed our lives to living the Jesus Path?"

Personally, I trust Jesus; I trust God and believe in God's grace and love. I trust that a loving God deals appropriately with those who commit evil. If these people are judged, I believe it's a judgment bringing repentance and remorse. Then they also will enter paradise. I do not believe in hell and I do not believe these people are cast into a dark separation from God. However, there are many followers of Jesus who strongly believe the evil ones will be cast into hell; but I don't. I believe I am just as guilty as those who committed murder. In the path that Manages our Shadow, Jesus taught that being angry with someone is no different than murdering them. I believe we are all equal before God at the moment of our death. If I enter paradise, then those who committed evil do so as well.

Some say what happens after we die is a great mystery. People who died and came back merely caught a glimpse of what happens. But I trust what Jesus said to the thief, *"Today you will be with me in paradise."* I believe the mystery of death is clarified—it is paradise.

Ultimately, we have no idea what paradise looks like. I can't give concrete answers to Lynn, Mitch, Carol, or all the others who asked me the same question. Many have said that I should just teach people to trust in God's love. But as I have said, I believe there is more. I give them my interpretation of Jesus's sentence: it happens immediately, our identities are not lost, we are not alone, and we need to trust that it is paradise.

Chapter Eleven: Walking the Paths

Once I took a pilgrimage to the Holy Land—Israel. The stories of Jesus that I had read about my entire life surrounded me. I'll never forget my early morning swim in the Sea of Galilee where Jesus grew up and began his ministry. During the swim, I was immersed in Jesus's presence—a dry sponge soaking up the water. The pilgrimage was a time of exploration and discovery. From the Mount of the Beatitudes to the city of Jerusalem, the stories of the Bible and the life of Jesus vibrated with meaning. The journey was a symphony for my soul. However, the pilgrimage was also a time of pain and turmoil. Sitting in the cell where it's believed Jesus spent his last night, I felt lost and alone like a child wandering through a dark forest. Walking the path where Jesus carried his cross to the mount of his crucifixion, I felt his despair and desperation. A pilgrimage takes you to spiritual heights as well as inviting you to explore the depths of your emotions and feelings. Following the Jesus Path is a pilgrimage. It can be a journey, a hike, a meander, or a climb. Whatever you call it, I invite you to engage in the adventure.

The study of the Jesus path is complete, and it is now your choice. You can close your e-Reader, put this book on a shelf, or your journey to follow Jesus can begin. This book wasn't written just to be read, but to be lived. I hope this book serves as a map and a guidebook for your journey.

How will you begin your pilgrimage? Which path will you choose to follow first? As someone who traversed this spiritual discovery, I have a few suggestions for your journey.

I encourage you to walk two paths simultaneously; the Path of the Bible and the Path of Prayer. Both paths start your pilgrimage down a well-paved road.

The Path of the Bible is as simple as going to a bookstore or downloading one for your reading tablet. I used the *New Revised Standard Version* for this book. I also recommend Eugene Peterson's translation called, *The Message*. Use my chapter on the Bible as your basic guide. Begin with the gospels, as they provide an overview of Jesus's life. As part of your journey, you may also enjoy practicing *Lectio Divina*, also mentioned in the Path of the Bible chapter.

To start the Path of Prayer, simply find a comfortable place to sit. Pay attention to your breathing and begin talking with God. Again, allow my chapter to be a basic guide to get you started.

After these paths, it's your choice on which path to follow next. I have two suggestions; you can take the path less traveled or take the path of least resistance. The path less traveled is one that is the least familiar. The chapter on Managing your Shadow may be unfamiliar, I encourage you to follow it for a few months and see what you learn.

It could be that you never thought about God's Will working through your life. You could commit to discerning this path as well, and again, see where God's Will takes you.

The path of least resistance is to choose a familiar one. Select a path where success is guaranteed. You may already be part of a community, but the Path of Community may encourage you to explore new ways to become more involved. Test the waters and dive in.

I encourage you to commit to a path for at least three months. This gives you plenty of time to explore, ask questions, and discover new insights.

Also, as you take different paths, it is important to consider which path gives you the most support. Since the Jesus Path can be confusing or overwhelming, it's good to have other travelers supporting you along the way. The Path of Community would provide this support. It may be helpful to join a group studying this book. You'll learn a great deal about each path by listening to those who share their own insights and ideas.

Eventually, you'll travel all paths simultaneously. You'll be reading the Bible and praying. As you encounter difficult situations, you'll contemplate the stream of God's Will. You'll become aware of your shadow and how to manage it. A loved one passes away, and you remember and find strength in the power of resurrection.

The paths weave together forming an expedition of faith. The further you travel on your spiritual pilgrimage, the more paths you may discover beyond the paths I shared. Here are other paths I considered including in this book.

- Path of the Ethical Life

- Path of Generosity

- Path of Sharing Your Faith

- Path of Church History

- Path of the Mind and Theology

Each path takes you further on your journey of spiritual discovery.

You'll also meet other pilgrims. Some are lost like a hiker floundering through the woods. When you encounter them, you can be a source of direction and guidance. Share this guidebook; encourage them on their journey.

Other pilgrims try to convince you that you're on the wrong path; your path is a dead end, or one that leaves you lost and alone. Smile when meeting these people. Don't try to argue or explain your journey, merely step to one side of the path, and let them pass. I've found arguing with them is like talking to someone with their ears plugged. You get nowhere, and it only delays your trek.

The important thing is to begin. Pack this book in your knapsack, pick up your walking stick, and begin the Pilgrimage of the Jesus Path.

I may meet you there.

Discussion Questions

Chapter One: My Story

- What's your story? How were you introduced to Jesus? Where you a child, a teenager, an adult?

- Did you have a dramatic experience of accepting Jesus at some point in your or did you always have a sense of following Jesus as a part of your faith development?

- How has your sense of following Jesus changed over the years?

- If you had to describe to someone why you follow Jesus what would you say?

Chapter Two: It Begins with Jesus

- What part of Jesus's life story surprises you most?

- Just as Jesus had family responsibilities that kept him from launching his ministry, what responsibilities do you have that keep you from fulfilling your dreams?

- Something happened in Jesus's life that finally released him to begin his ministry. What has happened in your own life that allowed you to pursue your dreams.

- What was it about the resurrection that compelled people to follow Jesus? Does it compel you? If so, how?

Chapter Three: The Path of Joy

- What brings you joy in life?

- Does your faith bring you joy?

- Why do you think Jesus was filled with Joy?

- Why are some christians so cranky?

- How do we find joy in the midst of difficult issues such as immigration, abortion, and gay marriage?

- How do we help others experience joy?

- Where is there joy in the midst of suffering for you?

- What do you think made Jesus laugh?

- What part of following Jesus makes you laugh? Or don't you laugh? If not, why are you taking your faith so seriously?

Chapter Four: The Path of the Bible

- Why do you think Jesus never wrote a book?

- Is the Bible holy for you? Why?

- What is your favorite Gospel? Why?

- What do you think this means, "The Gospel *according to . . .*"

- Is the inspiration of the Biblical authors greater or the same as the inspiration that guides people today?

- What does it mean to take the Bible seriously but not literally?

- Steve says we need to interpret the Bible. Which passages are the hardest for you to interpret?

- How do you apply the Bible to your life?

- What passages of the Bible have authority in your life?

- Which passages of the Bible are the hardest for you to understand?

- Have you ever read the Bible in the style of Lectio Divina

Chapter Five: The Path of God's Will

- Are you a strong-willed person? Is it hard for you to set aside what you want to do, and choose for what someone else wants you to do?

- If you were to describe to someone what God's will is, what would you say?

- What did Jesus mean when he said in the Lord's prayer, "Thy will be done on earth as it is in heaven?"

- How did Jesus choose for God's will?

- The chapter describes people who had to choose for God's will. When was there a time in your life when you had to discern God's will?

- Steve describes that the will of God is like a stream flowing down the side of a mountain. How do you understand this in your own life? What are the circumstances that have crashed into the stream of your life?

- When was there a time when your life imploded? How was God present during this time? How was God present in your life?

- Steve describes that there are times when God waits for us to choose a course of action, to exercise our will. When was there a time when God was waiting on you to choose?

- What does it mean to choose God's will when your life is at a junction? How do you discern God's will at this point?

- Steve mentions several biblical passages to help you discern God's will. Which is the most helpful for you?

- How do we choose God's will to benefit those who are oppressed? How do you do this in your life?

- How is death a part of God's will?

Chapter Six: The Path of Community

- Do you participate in a community of faith? Why do you do this?

- What are the benefits of being a part of a faith community? What are the challenges?

- The early church called them selves, "The Way." Why do you think they did this? Would you describe yourself as a part of the "Way?"

- The Apostle Paul used the metaphor for a body to describe the different roles people should fulfill in the church. Which part of a body would you say that you are?

- How does your faith community change the way people see God?

- Steve describes the being a part of a faith community means no one has to cry alone. When was there a time that you supported someone who was suffering? Maybe you were that person. Describe the experience.

- Why can there be so much conflict inside a church?

- Describe a time when you experienced conflict inside a church? How was it resolved?

- How does the word "conflict" make you feel? How well do you deal with conflict?

- How does God work through conflict?

- When Jesus said, "Where two or three are gathered in my name there I am also." How does this apply to your faith community?

- Is your faith community inclusive of all people? How is this a reflection of the teachings of Jesus?

Chapter Seven - The Path of Compassion

- What do you believe, is everyone saved, or only a few? Defend your position.

- Reflecting on Jesus parable are you a sheep or a goat?

- When was a time you showed compassion to the least of Jesus's brothers and sisters?

- Which do you believe is greater, to show compassion or have the right set of beliefs?

- How is forgiveness an expression of compassion?

- Who is someone you've had to forgive?

- Why is it so hard to forgive ourselves? How do we show compassion to ourselves?

- What does it mean to lose yourself? When have you lost yourself serving the needs of others?

- Jesus gives us a command to love one another, to show compassion. Why was this so important to Jesus?

- Who would you say is the least of Jesus brothers and sisters? How can you show compassion on them?

- Who do you know that is a living embodiment of compassion? How are they an example for you?

Chapter Eight: The Path of Prayer

- Who is someone in your life who has passed away that you ache to see again?

- Do you feel a similar ache to be with God?

- Does God ache to be with you?

- Did Jesus have an ache for God? Where do you see this ache in the Gospels?

- Do you feel the need to unplug from the noise of the world? How does this help you connect with God?

- How do you experience the presence of God? Through nature, the arts, science, through prayer? How are all these similar?

- What do you think about mantra's? Have you ever thought of using one? If you have one, what is it?

- Who taught you to pray?

- What are the things that you pray for?

- Have you ever had your prayers answered? What were they?

- Do you have a sacred space that you go to for prayer? Where is it? Describe it.

- Do you think prayer works? If so, how? If not, why not?

- Have you ever had to pray for your enemies? How did this change your perspective of this person?

- Describe how you pray. In this chapter Steve presents many teachings from Jesus about his view of prayer. Do these teachings shape your prayer life?

Chapter Nine: The Path of Managing the Shadow

- How do you feel about the word sin? Does this describe any part of your life?

- In the chapter Steve describes that sin draws us closer to God. How is this so?

- Steve describes that sin is like a dark goo in your life. Do you ever feel as though you get caught in this goo?

- God said to Paul, "My power is made perfect in your weakness." How is this true?

- Steve says that he struggles with the term, "Make a difference." How do you feel about his opinion? Do you agree or disagree?

- Steve describes that there are two forces in life, evil and live. How do you experience these two forces?

- What is your opinion about evil? How is it a reflection of sin? Who do you know has done something evil? Have you ever done something evil?

- What does it mean to baby step your way into evil?

- Do you believe in the devil? If so, how do you feel this presence in your life? If not, who do you describe the power that evil has in our lives?

- Steve shares his perspective of Jesus dying for our sins. What is your belief? Do you believe Jesus died for your sins? If so, why? If not, why not?

- How do you feel about the statement at the close of the chapter, "All shall be made well." Do you agree with this? How do you see God's power working until all shall be made well?

Chapter Ten: The Path of Resurrection

- In the opening section of the chapter Steve presents two people who approach their death. Who do you most identify with Jan or Alex?

- Do you believe Jesus's resurrection was physical or spiritual?

- Steve talks about the power of the resurrection moving through our lives. How do you feel this in your own life?

- Do you believe in heaven? What is your image of what it will be like.

- Steve describes an experience where he saw a soul lift from a body. Have you had similar experiences, or do you know of someone who has?

- Steve describes that after we die we will meet Jesus as he ushers us into what's next? Do you believe this? Do you find comfort in this?

- What is your view of paradise? How do you think your afterlife will be paradise?

- What do you believe about people who have committed great evil in life, the Hitlers, Stalins, etc. What do you believe happens to them after they die?

- Do you believe in hell? If so, does God condemn people to go there?

Chapter Eleven: Walking the Paths

- Which path for you will be the easiest to walk? Which path will be the most challenging?

- Steve mentions other paths to follow. Do any of those intrigue you?

- What do you do when you meet people on your pilgrimage that disagree with what you believe?

- What do you think? Are you going to walk the Jesus Path?